THE DAY GUINEA REJECTED DE GAULLE OF FRANCE AND CHOSE INDEPENDENCE

THE DAY GUINEA REJECTED DE GAULLE OF FRANCE AND CHOSE INDEPENDENCE

LANSINÉ KABA
with assistance from Stephen Belcher

This book is a publication of
Diasporic Africa Press
NEW YORK | WWW.DAFRICAPRESS.COM
Copyright @ Diasporic Africa Press 2020

All rights reserved. No part of this publication may be reproduced or distributed in any form or
by any means, or stored in a database or retrieval system, without the prior written permission of
the publisher.

ISBN-13 978-1-937306-72-4 (pbk.: alk paper)

LCCN: 2020939769

Printed in the United States of America on acid-free paper.

TABLE OF
CONTENTS

DEDICATION

To my son, Ali-Moussa, and to his age-mates, in the hope that they will grow up, will learn, and will live in liberty, with honor and compassion.

To my uncles, Sékou Diané and Nara-Madi Diané, Kaba-Laye, and Diafodé Kaba; to my friends Ismael Nabé, Paul Stephen, and Fadel Ghussein: they all were either executed, hung, or died in detention after November 1970; to my uncle, Ba-Karamoko, and to my brother, N'Fa Mory Kaba, who died in detention in 1984 and 1986; and to all the victims of the oppression and the repression, with the wish that liberty, concord, and prosperity may flourish in Guinea.

To the memory of my uncle, Al-Hadji Djankanagbè-N'Faly Kaba, a preeminent figure in Kankan during the 1950s; to my sister, Hadja Djankana, a lady of charm, beauty, and virtue, keen in wit and pious, and who would have wished to know how to read and write; to my friend, Professor Sékéné-Mody Cissoko of Dakar, and then leading guru in Bamako; and to Fanta, my wife and devoted friend.

This book is also dedicated to the memory of Professor Ibrahima Baba Kaké, who died in Paris on July 7, 1994; he suggested writing it.

In the memory of my cousin Mamadi Diané, businessman in Washington D.C., who died in Abidjan, Côte d'Ivoire, August 24, 2020.

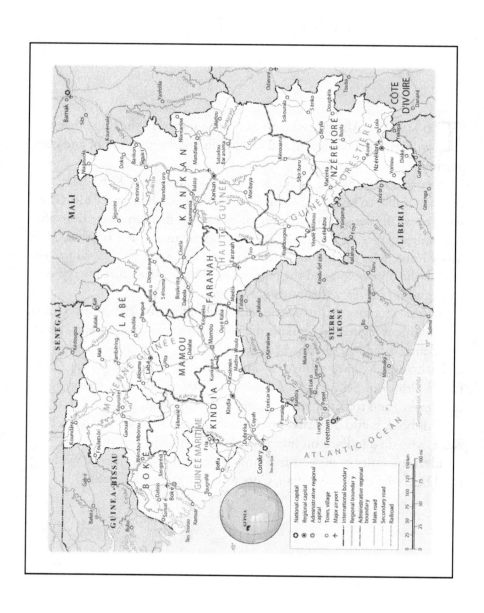

FOREWORD

T HESE FIRST PARAGRAPHS shine a previously unpublished light on the original Preface I wrote when this book first appeared in French in 1989. How fortunate that a text, now some years old, has preserved its relevance! This occurrence confirms the idea that questions relating to broad subjects such as political reform, independence, constitution, identity, culture, or dignity are of interest to readers from any generation. To some extent, everyone has some curiosity about the history of their country and their family.

The original book, *Le Non de la Guinée*, has been reprinted several times under the title *Le Non de la Guinée à de Gaulle*, before Professor Baba Kaké, editor of the series *Afrique contemporaine* (Contemporary Africa), and I terminated our respective contracts with the Chaka Publishing House in Paris and in Dakar. It is worth repeating here that I am still grateful for the respect Kaké showed me. I am also delighted by the confidence of the readers who have acquired copies of the book, and I would readily and gratefully acknowledge that some readers, in writing or in person, have shared their opinions with me. Thanks to them, the book has had a certain success, and I admit a debt to them.

This work examines one of the great questions in French history, with that of its tropical dependencies in the mid-20TH century, and specifically in the mid-1950s. Guinea occupied a singular place therein. France emerged from the war, anemic because of the trials of the lengthy global conflict. For some years, she offered the impression of recovery, in a haphazard pattern. But in truth, all the signs indicated further weaknesses and decline. The aftermath of the war and the cost of the conflicts erupting in the colonies devoured the State's finances and increased its dependence on loans. From the start of 1958, the government was trying to resolve the continuing effects of the latest crisis of the Fourth Republic, particularly the public finances, the Algerian struggle, and the lack of political stability and coherent and efficient diplomacy. These matters affected the progress of the country and of its overseas territories and were the subject of general discussion.

No one can change or reshape the great events of history. In this case, the events that occurred in 1958 are inflexible, immutable, and inalterable. These events left their mark on the people of France and her colonies. This is one reason why any revision of the original text of this book can only be limited and sober. The revision cannot affect the basis of the work; no more than history can be redone or repeated. An author, on the other hand, may always review their interpretations of facts or the understanding of the characters; the author may also reconsider the way he expressed his thoughts. That is what I undertake in the present version of the text, with full recognition that it does not constitute a new work.

When in December of 1987, my fellow-countryman, Prof. Ibrahima Baba Kaké asked me for a contribution with a book dealing with Guinea's vote in the Referendum of September 28, 1958, couched in terms accessible to the general reader, I hesitated. I felt no qualms about describing a major event in contemporary history to an informed public. I felt no apprehension in dealing with a subject that continues to be a burning issue, involving fascinating and controversial personalities. I am well-acquainted with the questions of Guinean history, from the pre-colonial era to the current regime. History is my passion.

Why did I hesitate? I hesitated because contemporary history is not to be confused with politics, and I did not want to engage in politicking. History does not require an ideological position, nor philosophical theses, nor great theoretical orations. Instead, it requires a great rigor in the analysis of the actions and the behaviors of people, commoners, and leaders alike. I had other reasons to hesitate as well: to speak of the referendum in Guinea did not seem simple. To start with, the question involved France herself, her government, and her institutions, that since 1945, had been deficient and lacking, so much as to seem on their deathbed. The topic was not at all simple. It involved, of course, the Fourth Republic, with its weaknesses and contradictions. It also offered an "antithesis" of de Gaulle's return to power, and the establishment of the Fifth Republic. This question is of concern to savants, historians, and those interested in politics and development.

Sékou Touré

Many facets of this issue involve sub-Saharan Africa, specifically the creation of the Republic of Guinea, my native land, and the development of the myths around its founding president, Sékou Touré. He is remembered as the African who dared to challenge the great Charles de Gaulle. The topic remains critical, capital, and always meaningful and interesting. How should one describe such a grand and striking movement as the Referendum of 1958, especially as it applied in Guinea? The movement was loaded with a powerful and extraordinary force, rare and almost unique within the annals of the decolonization of tropical Africa. And— surprise of surprises—the event quickly gave birth to a new state in a Black Africa that was then under colonial dominion. This new state also quickly produced a political regime: glorious at its start, affirmed and approved by most, but over time, it became controversial, lugubrious, and even in some regard, disapproved. The régime and the actions of the *Parti démocratique de Guinée* (PDG: Democratic party of Guinea) quickly aroused as much pride as shock and dismay. In France, the referendum led to the Fifth Republic and its great achievements, which have transformed the contours of contemporary France.

First, the event of the Referendum, strictly speaking, took place well beyond the limits of Guinea, and to a far lesser extent compared to the French Soudan (Mali) or the colony of Niger. Those involved in the Referendum were mainly the French in France, the France of the "Hexagon," as it was later called, then the *dépendences d'outre-mer* (French territories outside Europe) that were, of course, by constitutional law, considered parts of France. The Referendum precipitated a series of events throughout this political entity, from the core Hexagon into the colonies. The independence of Guinea came about within that general context, and the example of Guinea quickly encouraged the French territories in west and equatorial Africa (along with Madagascar, which is further away) to negotiate their own terms of independence without any great procrastination.

Nor should the historian underestimate the almost umbilical and maternal links that thus, from the perspective of history, link the origins of the Fifth French Republic and the Republic of Guinea. Those bonds, in the best of all possible worlds, might have proved the basis for Franco-Guinean friendship. Although both entities are now separated, might we recognize that they both resulted from the consequences of the same constitutional reform that was advocated, in different ways, by the citizens of the Fourth French Republic and by those of Guinea? The plan for reforms that was announced in the spring of 1958, as history shows, disrupted political life on the banks of the Seine through the following months and into autumn. His electoral victory everywhere—save in Guinea—allowed General Charles de Gaulle and his team to settle a number of significant problems in the French state: 1) to establish a new constitution for the Fifth Republic, and 2) immediately after the Referendum vote, to ignore Sékou Touré and to reject the Franco-African community of Guinea. In my opinion, this point deserves to be stressed. The history of Franco-Guinean relations, despite the tensions experienced over the past thirty years, serve to confirm this point.

General Charles de Gaulle

In short, the vast topic was enticing, or even irresistible, for someone with a sense of the history. In the context of plans for this book, there was no difficulty in explaining the position taken in Paris by General Charles de Gaulle, the former president of the provisional government of the Republic, appointed in 1945, and then quickly defeated in the corridors of the Palais Bourbon in January of 1946. He felt it was imperative and urgent to define the functions of the governmental authorities and assemblies through a text in clear and precise language. In the spring of 1958, de Gaulle clung to his old plan for a constitutional law, called the Bayeux plan, and remained committed to the idea of a strong constitution and a solid state to steer France in the concert of the great modern nations that emerged after the Second World War, among whom France found a permanent seat in the Security Council of the United Nations. The same passion moved him at a time of agitation on both sides of the Mediterranean. This came in the process of decolonization, after the humiliating defeat of the French army on the plains of Dien Bien Phu in Vietnam, in the very crux of a crisis in Tunisia and of the war in Algeria. France faced grave and troublesome problems within and without her borders. De Gaulle felt that immediate action was required.

Furthermore, it was difficult to judge the maturity of the colonized African people of Guinea, specifically that of their principal leader, Sékou Touré, and his party, the PDG. Touré had transformed a labor movement into a party of the masses, demanding social action. It spread and eventually, it dominated the entire country. His seizure of power started gradually in 1957, and then became absolute and lasted until his death in 1984. By 1988, everyone knew how his regime had endowed Guinea with its fundamental institutions and defended its independence from real and imagined enemies. At first, well-liked and popular, the regime gradually turned to arbitrary policies. The country became the symbol of a strong and hard despotism.

Surprisingly, barely a week after the death of Sékou Touré in March of 1984, he was replaced by a military government led by Colonel Lansana Conté. In other words, according to observers, the regime of the PDG seemed to have failed in many respects. The question is still open, however, as to whether their failures justified the putsch of April 6, 1984. Public opinion is divided on the matter. The historian's problem is to avoid the pitfalls of subjectivity. For us Guinea remains the principal topic of the work: it was the territory that dared reply "NO" to the call of General de Gaulle in 1958. I will take note of the actions of the leaders and the people, of the parties and of other groups, in short, of the whole human ensemble that constituted the colony of Guinea.

For the historian, it is a matter of distinguishing between what is known now, in the present, and that which no one might have anticipated or suspected in 1958. Nowadays, observers from many perspectives will readily speak of the failure of the PDG's actions on many levels. However, in 1958, at the time of Independence, such statements would have been impossible. In 1958, Guinea faced the unknown, the impossibility of foretelling what the nation might accomplish under Touré and his team, and the imponderable dream of Guineans for the happier future announced on the radio and in the propaganda. Such distinctions required patient work in dispassionate analysis and reconstruction, setting aside ideological or ethnic perspectives. For my part, this meant that whatever judgment one wished to make on Guinea under Sékou Touré, or on the leader himself and his associates, I had to resist the temptation of projecting the present into the future. This is a mistake made by many critics of the PDG, in the past and in the present. I explained to Kaké that I needed to place the event of 1958 in its own terms, to situate the Referendum in its global and contemporary historical context. Only such a focus would allow me to discern the face of the actors, and to present them as they were seen in 1958, instead of the way they were seen in the 1970s, a period of "plots," or later, in the late 1980s, when the country faced new problems.

I also felt that any study of the Referendum could not be an ordinary historical or political kind of analysis. It neither could nor limit itself to a mere rehearsal of the legend of the PDG and of its founder. The work should not consist in a historical review of French colonization nor of the African nationalism of Guinea. In my view, that day—September 28, 1958—represented a unique moment, a specific event that proved extraordinary and fateful for the history both of France and Guinea. Viewed in its proper light, it symbolized the phenomenon of the hatching of the independent nation of Guinea in the days between August 25 and October 2 of 1958.

The Referendum of September 28, 1958 was a crucial and decisive event. It involved the action of the great figures, and then engaged in their professions and causes. It was a way to make a statement on the part of the populations of France and of Guinea. This majestic movement carried Guinea onto unexpected and uncertain paths. The event was indisputably the culmination of a great range of hopes and thoughts, the result of a deep self-examination in which individual perspectives as well as religious, cultural, and social forces had an effect across the full extent of the national territory, without the "ethnicism that would later emerge." In Guinea, the movement of 1958 may stand for a fine example of the birth of a national sentiment, without hate or prejudice. Guineans of all ethnicities and faiths dreamed of the birth of a New World, of peace, well-being, and gentle fraternity.

It would be a great mistake to omit from a tally of the great figures of the Guinean epos the names of the historical leaders of the opposition to the PDG. True, these leaders had been defeated—one might even say humiliated—in the elections of 1956. However, without their patriotism and their wisdom, Guinea might have gone the way of Niger under Bakari Djibo. Hence, the success of the Referendum lies not only at the feet of the PDG-RDA, whose role is indisputable, but also, to some extent, with all the other political organizations, the unions, the student associations, as well as women. The vote demonstrated this consensus. The leaders of the *Bloc africain de Guinée* (BAG: African Bloc of Guinea) proved able to behave as the loyal opposition and to join in communal action with Touré and his party. They, and all the people of Guinea, are worthy of honor for their accomplishment.

Obviously, among the many leaders, Sékou Touré—*Sily* (in the Susu language), the "Elephant of Guinea"—deserved the choice place. In 1958, he incarnated the aspirations of the people in many regards. The tones of his strong voice echoed across the lands, announcing the dawn of a New Era under the guidance of his party. The epic that later became the tragedy of Guinea can be identified, without exaggeration, with his personality—one that was both simple and complex. And again, how might one explain the Referendum with any mention of the saga of General Charles de Gaulle in France? He must be mentioned, be one Gaullist or not. De Gaulle stands in French history as the man of the 18TH of June. He was the prodigious French patriot of that time, the leader of the Cross of Lorraine, the man broke with Marshal Pétain, the man who called himself the "living symbol of hope for France." After the lightning-swift defeat of the French armies by the Nazi forces, it was de Gaulle, exiled in London, who, on June 18, 1940, launched a call to France for a national resistance. De Gaulle organized and led the great movement of liberation that waged the struggle across the French territory, including North, West, and Equatorial Africa. He gained recognition by the Allies, meaning the US, England, Canada, and the USSR, as the leader of the Free French. In 1944, in Brazzaville (Congo), de Gaulle proclaimed the necessity of introducing reforms into the colonial system and of changing the manner of governance. He wished to reform France and give his fellow-citizens lessons in civic duty, in politics, in involvement, and in history.

De Gaulle wondered what was preventing the French state from operating properly and from fulfilling its potential. On this question, he followed the example of many public intellectuals or political leaders, such as Maurice Thorez, Pierre Mendès-France, François Mauriac, Albert Camus, Jacques Soutelle, Michel Debré, André Malraux, and many others. The list is heterogeneous. He opined in his own fashion and managed to convince some.

The answer went directly, foremost, to the excessive parliamentarianism of the constitution of 1945, and secondarily, to the very inconsistency of the French, their versatile or even capricious and uncertain tendencies. This issue led to another: why didn't the Parliament itself, and freely, change the constitutional articles that restrained the government's operation? These questions led to his conviction that a total, absolute reform of the institutions of the Republic was necessary. These considerations were part of the Gaullist doctrine. Gaullism sought to control the times during and after the World War in France. During the period, immediately following the end of the war, the opinions of the voters crystalized around the issues of supplies, housing, health, transportation, schooling, and communications. The political world rapidly resumed its course, with its old divisions and new ones that had come out of the war. Those issues marked the choices and the political positions. Despite having a character that transcended party loyalty, de Gaulle could not overcome the currents of protest and division. While offering the impression that it comprehended nationalism and socialism—the doctrines then in fashion—Gaullisme was opposed to disorder in any of its forms and sought, as much as possible, a union of all the active forces in society.

De Gaulle's great role during the war years earned him the presidency of the provisional government of the Republic, but he had no true political organization to support him other than the vast national movement known as the *Rassemblement du peuple français* (RPF). Like so many of the other parties and groups of the period, the movement had no ideological cohesion or tangible structures. The RPF attracted many supporters and partisans of variable tendencies and won many votes during the elections. However, the alliance of the communists and the socialists established a majority in the Parliament. De Gaulle disliked political divisions, and specifically the idea of governing in a parliamentary system. He, therefore, faced a dilemma.

Helped by Michel Debré, and to demonstrate his desire to reform institutions, in October 1945, he established the *École nationale d'administration* (ENA), an elite and superior national school whose graduates would serve in the various branches of the public and private administration. This school, the first among the great schools, would be, borrowing the terms of the writer, Jean-Michel Gaillard, "the prestigious mirror of the state and might manage to harmonize the practices of many large offices." However, some months later, in January of 1946, de Gaulle resigned from the government, and in 1955, even decided to disband the RPF. These actions confirmed the dilemma of his political position, but they did not mark the end of his involvement. The General still preserved his vision for a constitutional reform, and he awaited the propitious moment to return to the stage.

In 1958, after years of self-imposed exile in his property of Colombey-les-deux-églises in Lorraine, de Gaulle benefited from a conjunction of events. At that point, the army of Algeria arrogated the right to intervene directly in a border dispute with Tunisia, and on February 8TH attacked the village of Sakiet-Sidi-Youssef, perhaps without orders from the Prime Minister Félix Gaillard (the matter remained unresolved). The bombardment caused dozens of casualties and wounded in the training camp of the Algerian National Liberation Front (FLN), as well as in the marker and the primary school of the small town. Habib Bourguiba, president of Tunisia, brought the matter to international attention, and presented a complaint to the Security Council of the United Nations.

France was forced to receive a Mission of "Good Service" from the international organizations. The right, in the Palais Bourbon, interpreted this fact as a humiliation and a betrayal. The Algerian situation was becoming an international issue, very close to the problem of Indo-China some years before. This Tunisian border issue was compounded with problems due to the endemic weakness of public finance in the French state, and its continual dependence on the United States and its need for loans. The imbroglio eventually led to the fall of Félix Gaillard's government.

The parliamentary crisis demonstrated, once again, the inherent weaknesses of the system of the Fourth Republic. No party, no political coalition, no major figure in the National Assembly proved able to form a governing team to resolve the crisis. The situation was further embroiled by the threats of the unions, by protests from the groups of students, and counter-protests from groups on the right. Tensions were increasing rapidly in Algeria, on the other side of the Mediterranean, particularly in the towns of Algiers and Oran, driven by extremist forces and by the officers of the right. Civil war was a threat. In these circumstances, President René Coty called on General de Gaulle to establish a solid and stable government, and to muffle the voices of mutiny; Coty considered de Gaulle as the most "illustrious of the French." We shall return to this point later.

De Gaulle left an undeniable mark on his country and its colonies. Well before 1958, going back to the time of the Resistance during WWII and after the liberation of France, he represented an unchallenged and irresistible force, as we have suggested above. He managed to appeal to most of the active movements in the country, and for a time, to cooperate with them, and then to withdraw from the "politicians' policies of the Fourth Republic," despite his exceptional talents as an orator and debater. Even during his voluntary exile, the shadow—for some, the halo—of the General loomed over the land and weighed upon it. A movement swiftly crystalized in his name, made up of the discontent, the protesters of various tendencies, all driven by the desire to renew the order of things. After May 13, 1958, the name of de Gaulle became the source of the Referendum, and later, the force behind the spirit of renovation, called to transform from top to bottom the physiognomy of France, from its administration to its industries, its finances, and its foreign relations. He became incontestably the founding father of the Fifth Republic and of the renovation that France has undergone since 1958.

There is a symbiotic relationship between individuals and their nations, although the life of peoples is not the same as that of persons. Great figures sometimes affect a part of the history of their society, and in so doing, help to lead them toward summits or toward the abyss. Therefore, such great figures like de Gaulle in 1940 and in 1958 might claim that they have changed history and present themselves as the living awareness of their country. A historian is interested in such events.

The events of the 1950s, in France as well as in her colonies, should be interpreted with consideration given to the interaction of the institutions of government, the elected representatives, and the constituent population, regarding the notions of power, security, and prosperity. More specifically, in Guinea, the struggles between the parties, the competition between labor movements, and the numerous riots, in Conakry and in the interior, were centered on nothing but the control and exercise of authority, the right to make decisions, to distribute resources in a proper manner, and hence, to oversee, organize, chastise, and reward in the name of the people.

In Conakry, a moderate trio—Diawadou Barry, Framoï Bérété, Karim

Bangoura—with their allies of noble origin from the main regions of the country were struggling against another trio—Touré, Diallo, Béavogui—that was dynamic, engaged, and activist, but that also, in its own manner, was not without claims to noble status. Their partisans presented themselves as closer to, and in better understanding, with the deprived groups. To resume: in Guinea, the power in politics showed a relationship with a small group of people who did, or wished to, detain power, and the wider group of the people who were the true source of power. This was the essence of the political situation. The government derived its vital force from this dynamic. The same held true across the Franco-African collective.

During the spring of 1958, political issues presented themselves sharply, in France as well as in Guinea. In Paris, the attention of Parliament was turned particularly to social and fiscal issues, examined also by politicians, financiers, and technocrats. These were so numerous and influential that it was easy to imagine that France was governed by law firms and consultancies. Paris needed a sizeable loan from Washington to support its finances. Further, the Algerian crisis was becoming more and more serious, with military and diplomatic ramifications.

For instance, as was noted above, the government of Tunisia was quick to protest French operations on its border, where the Algerian FLN had, for some time, maintained a military base. And still at the start of the year 1958, a problem broke out in Sakiet Sidi Youssef, a distant place in Tunisia near the border with Algeria. In an attack, the French air force caused many deaths, injuries and material destruction. The Tunisian president, Habib Bourguiba, informed the United Nations Security Council of this matter in February. This infraction of the borders poisoned relations between Paris, Tunis, and Cairo, seat of the Arab League. It also negatively affected the relations between the French Prime Minister and the military command in Algeria. The crisis would soon come to a point.

After May 13, 1958, when de Gaulle, as had been expected, took power, the question of renewal became ever more important in the current agenda. The issue spread in its immediacy, involving France and her colonial possessions. For France was not merely an ancient nation with a prestigious place in history; she was also a power at the heart of the North Atlantic Treaty Organization (NATO), and of the European Economic Community. She was a state offering considerable opportunity for international influence. De Gaulle's heartfelt dream was to seize power and to promote the resurgence of "his" France, to consolidate the bonds between himself, who had the ideas and gave orders in the name of the French, that those who would execute his orders to fulfill the goal of renewal (with or without the overseas territories).

One might compare the General's program and actions, product of a political perspective, with the great nationalist current that since the Second World War, had been roiling the colonized people. Many indications suggest that de Gaulle, the patriot, could understand African nationalism in general, and even the Guinean version. His meeting with Sékou Touré, on August 25 in Conakry, would help to clarify points, one way or another.

In theory, nationalism involved several feelings and movements. These various manifestations aimed at an extension of rights and duties, at participation, and at the emancipation of the communities in political matters. They stipulated, to some degree, a recognition of the identity of the populations and of their cultures; this amounted to reclaiming parts of national power and sovereignty. From a historical perspective, nationalism illustrated two clear and specific points: first, it involved, in past times, an end to monarchism, to the privileges and claims of groups of unequal rank and status. Second, nationalism gave birth to a world of citizens who were free and equal in the land or their birth or their adopted country. One of the principles of nationality derives from these points.

Nationalism evokes an exaltation of the spirit of association and cooperation, and of unity among the members of a given territory or a given community, in service to a common political purpose. The republican nationalist principle first emerged in the North American republic of 1776, although the idea had been found in the writings of philosophers of the Enlightenment in Europe. Thereafter, it spread with the French Revolution across Europe during the 19TH century, as one of those great unseen forces that moves people. Colonization brought it, unintentionally, in its baggage to Africa. Then the independence movements grew out of it and amplified its resonance.

Nationalist thought, as expressed by Sékou Touré in 1958, involved ideas of liberty, of independence, of sovereignty, of dignity, of unity, of progress, along with the idea of anti-colonialism. Gaullism, a movement grounded in a respect for order, for the land of one's birth, and the injustices of Naziism, might have, in its own way, grasped the legitimacy of the ardent complaints of African nationalists such as Sékou Touré. However, was it not the personal issues during the debate in the Territorial Assembly in Conakry, on August 25, that precluded this dialogue? Our later analysis will demonstrate this point. Thus, nationalist discourse defines itself easily as a weapon that may lead to regrettable consequences.

Speeches such as those uttered during the Assembly in Conakry, expressed rigid viewpoints. Touré and de Gaulle engaged through their language. It was often calculated, at times spontaneous, and prideful, and so made for difficult listening. Their words, however, presented solemn truths that were difficult to reconcile. In short, impulsiveness prevented the possibility of a dialogue. Therein lies the tragedy of August 25TH and the Franco-Guinean divorce that would endure for generations. The reputation of General de Gaulle was confirmed. The myth of Sékou Touré as the great, bold champion of liberation also took form on that date.

Under those conditions, as I explained to Kaké, any study of the Referendum of September 1958, had to involve a general view of the whole of Guinea, as well as the consideration of France. The critical and decisive moment certainly looks to the consolidation of power by the PDG after the passage of the constitutional law of May 1957. However, that privileged moment also extends to May 13, 1958, the date of the establishment of the new Gaullist government, and to October 2, 1958, the date on which the independence of Guinea was formally declared. It is within this short and critical period that we must explore the underside of the constitutional and political operations in Paris, and lay bare the maneuvering of the different parties, and present the social and cultural forces and Guinea's economic potential: in short, to reveal the epic actions that would give birth to a new nation.

The breadth of this historical reconstruction, and the time limits allotted for the work, justified my hesitations after Kaké sent me the book proposal. However, a visit to Guinea in December 1988, proved most useful to me. I could talk with witnesses, with long-time members of the PDG, and with professors. All this encouraged me to accept the invitation to write. The more so as the vote of September 28, the symbol of a definite national consensus, counts among the memorable pages—and why shouldn't we even say, glorious—of the history of modern Guinea. Even a short book may cast light on the deep sources for the origin of the nation.

We should offer some comments on the sources. History requires data, be they written or oral. This work is based, in part, on sources that I assembled during my vacations while I was a student at the Sorbonne, from witnesses in Guinea in the period 1959-63. It also relies upon information I acquired, and on my personal experience in Kankan and in Conakry during the first years of the 1950s. The written documentation on Guinea offers the semblance of a great abundance. Many Governors of *la France d'outre-mer* (overseas territories), researchers of various nationalities, and some journalists have provided writings on subjects relating to Guinean politics. Their information is useful and interesting, but sometimes unfair and rushed on the period of the Referendum. While on this topic, it seems opportune to recognize the work of Guinean professors and writers. Few, alas, have put their work into writing. Despite their differences in ideology, in training, or in temperament, these authors have turned their attention to the problems of their country. And so, they write, as might be expected, as participants and as observers. Since we will be quoting them later, as appropriate, we should note the writings of Laye Camara, Alpha Condé, Charles Diané, Sylvain S. Camara, Sidiki Kéita, and Ibrahima Baba Kaké, among many others.

What a service to future generations might have been made had the literate participants in the era of political struggles and the regime of the PDG chosen to record their observations! The exception here is the former minister and dignitary of the PDG (before he was sent to prison), Alpha-Abdoulaye Diallo, a learned and brilliant lawyer, and his book *La vérité du ministre*. Writing in his capacity as a former dignitary, and later, a critic of the PDG, Diallo describes the defensive circling of the wagons in Guinea that came about after the Portuguese invasion on November 22, 1970. President Sékou Touré was gifted with an undeniable sense of history, and as he loved writing, he left many philosophical treatises for posterity. Alas, the president, a scrupulous witness, was content to offer his observations and his speeches, without preserving for posterity his impressions of historical events and personalities. We know full well that speeches, whatever their value, are often lifeless, devoid of pertinent detail. The historian's duty is to probe this pile of ideas and passions, in their philosophical and sociological tones, to capture the personality of the speaker and the movement of history. Further, we might expect that an organized party, such as the PDG, would possess its own archives.

There was great disappointment among the historians interested in the nationalist movement in Guinea, in the period 1947-1984, to hear the news of a systematic destruction of the archives of the PDG's Political Office after the coup d'état of April 1984.

While it is brought to fruit through personal initiative, any book also draws upon the knowledge or the participation of many other persons, more than may be acknowledged. I would give thanks for their help to numerous persons, starting with my uncle, El-Hadj N'Faly Kaba, chairman of the BAG of Kankan up to 1958, his friends, my great-uncle, the well-known scholar, Karamo-Talibi Kaba, my aunt, Hadja Nyamakoron Kaba, one of the first women involved with the PDG-RDA in Kankan, and continuing with my brother, Mana-Diafodé Kaba, Director of the National Office for Hydrocarburants in Kankan, and my friend, Cheick Chérif, former Director of Radio-Conakry and former Ambassador to Moscow. Ibrahima B. Kaké was exceptionally helpful, sharing a portion of his copious research materials with me. My book could not have been completed within the deadline without the help and the application of my assistants, Joel Uriodain and Myriam Pauillac, and in Chicago of my secretaries, Jennifer Boyd and Mildred Snell.

Finally, a last word to Fanta Traoré, my dear wife and companion. While caring for our still-young son, Ali-Moussa, she helped me through all the stages of the production of the text, often into the late hours of the night. Without her help, the intellectual marathon from which this book sprouted could never have been accomplished. Once again, and writing now from Doha in the month of May 2020, I would say I am more than thankful to her, and give the last word on the book to its readers.

A TIMELINE
OF EVENTS

1946, May: Constitution of the PDG (Parti démocratique de Guinée: Democratic Party of Guinea), the Guinean chapter of the RDA.

1946, October: A Congress establishes the RDA (*Rassemblement démocratique african*: African Democratic Alliance).

1953, May: The French army suffers a great defeat at Dien Bien Phu in north Vietnam.

1953, August: Sékou Touré is elected as Member of the Territorial Council for Beyla.

1953, November: End of the 70-day strike led by Sékou Touré.

1954, June: Founding of the political party, the BAG (*Bloc africain de Guinée*: African Bloc of Guinea), by Framoï Bérété, Diawadou Barry, Karim Bangoura, and the election of Diawadou Barry as *député* following the death of Yacine Diallo.

1956, January: Sékou Touré and Saifoulaye Diallo are elected as *députés*.

1956, June: The National Assembly in Paris adopts the Loi cadre, known as the Loi Defferre, governing the internal autonomy of the colonial territories.

1956, November: Sékou Touré is elected Mayor of Conakry.

1957, March: The PDG is triumphant in the territorial elections, and Sékou Touré is elected Chair of the Council of Government, under the Loi cadre (Loi cadre for decolonization).

1957, March: Kwame Nkrumah and his party wins independence for the British colony of the Gold Coast, that takes the name of Ghana.

1957, September: Third Congress of the RDA in Bamako, and a gathering of the PDG in January 1958.

1958, January: The government, under the fundamental law, abolishes traditional chieftaincy in Guinea.

1958, January: A Congress establishes the UGTAN (*Union générale des travailleurs d'Afrique noire*: General Union of Workers in Black Africa) in Conakry.

1958, May: Riots by the French burst out in Algiers.

1958, May: Bloody confrontations in Conakry.

1958, June: Establishment of de Gaulle's government, revision of constitutional laws. Sékou Touré is kept out of the Constitutional Consultative Committee.

1958, July: Presentation of the draft of the constitutional project to the Constitutional Consultative Committee, and debates on the Federal Executive.

1958, July: A special meeting of the Territorial Assembly in Conakry; a gathering of the PRA (*Parti du regroupement africain*: Party of African Union) in Cotonou.

1958, August 5: De Gaulle receives Sékou Touré, speaking for the RDA.

1958, August 8: De Gaulle gives a sharp and threatening speech to the Constitutional Consultative Committee in Paris.

1958, August 9: Sékou Touré answers de Gaulle.

1958, August 19: Start of de Gaulle's tour through Madagascar and French colonies in Africa.

1958, August 25: De Gaulle arrived in Conakry; he and Touré give two major speeches in the hall of the Territorial Assembly in Conakry.

1958, August 27: Conversations between Sékou Touré and Bernard Cornut-Gentille, Minister, in Dakar.

1958, August 28: A joint declaration by Sékou Touré, Bakari Djibo of

Niger, and Abdoulaye Diallo from Soudan (Mali) against the Referendum.

1958, August 29: At the invitation of President Pouech of the Chamber of Commerce of Conakry, Sékou Touré gives a speech intended to reassure the Europeans of Guinea.

1958, September 7: Death of the *député* Ouezzin Coulibaly in Paris; Sékou Touré does not attend his funeral held in Bobo-Dioulasso (Upper Volta/Burkina Faso) on September 15.

1958, September 14: A large territorial conference about the Referendum.

1958, September 28: Guinea votes NO to the Referendum.

1958, September 29: Special Envoy Risterucci delivers a note from the French government announcing that French civil servants would be recalled and that aid to Guinea would be suspended.

1958, October 2: Guinea proclaims itself independent.

CHAPTER 1
DE GAULLE TAKES POWER

THE RUPTURE IN relations between Guinea and France, the advent of the French Fifth Republic, and the independence of African states following that of Guinea: all these events, to some degree, were influenced by the consequences of the events of May 13, 1958, in Algiers and in Paris. In the past three years, France had undergone a crisis, due inherently to the purely parliamentary system of the government of the Fourth Republic. In that system, the state was led by the chairman of a council—the head of the government or a prime minister—accompanied by members of government chosen by the parties. Cabinets included technical and political counselors. The prime minister held most of the power, but his authority was dependent upon agreement among the parties whose alliance would make or break the government. Any swift change within the majority of the *Chambre des députés* (House of Representatives)—as occurred during the recent crisis over Sakiet-Sidi-Youssef—became a deadly shoal in the course of the Fourth Republic.

Furthermore, the question of the colonies, that once had been a matter of national prestige, had now become a challenging and dangerous issue. After the French defeat at Dien Bien Phu in Vietnam/Tonkin in 1953 (it became the symbol of problems within the army), the matter of colonial wars haunted the minds of the political leaders and undermined the regime. Then came Morocco and Tunisia—further troublesome reminders. No party leader proved strong enough to offer a solution. The war in Algeria was particularly upsetting and critical. Lying across the Mediterranean, Algeria was counted among the *départements* (administrative districts) and thus, was included as part of the Hexagon, the name given to the territory of France. French colonial settlers in Algeria went back to the 1830s, when the territory was conquered; the settlers were known as *Pieds-noirs* (black feet).

However, it was just as much a colony comprised of indigenous peoples— Amazigh and Arab Muslims who were exploited and oppressed. After February 1956, when Guy Mollet, Chairman of the Council, was attacked by Algerians of European origin because his policies were considered too liberal toward the Muslims, passions became inflamed. A rupture between Paris and the Algerian colonists seemed inevitable. Conditions became even more serious after the army illegally seized Ahmed Ben Bella and other leaders of the FLN (the National Liberation Front). The Front extended its control over urban and rural populations and was proving to be the most popular movement among the Muslim Algerians. More and more clearly, the Expeditionary Corps and its officers showed their distance from the government and demanded greater freedom in conducting their war against the forces struggling for liberation, hoping to restore the shine to their escutcheon, tarnished by the defeat in Vietnam at Dien Bien Phu. Veterans believed that the army was frustrated of its victory and was the victim of the politicians. All these factors pointed to a conflict whose end was obvious: The state would be discomfited and national confidence would be shattered by the disorders. The situation in Algeria was a powder-keg at risk of explosion, with serious and unforeseen consequences.

The political situation turned sharply toward the worst. The instability threatened the survival of the regime. As confirmation of these various fears, a new ministerial crisis burst out on April 15, 1958. Felix Gaillard's government, bled white by deep and irreversible disagreement, fell to the combined blows of the right, that considered it too bold on the Algerian question, and of the left, that considered it rather timid. Thus, the government was the target of choice, and the victim of the morbidity that afflicted that regime. In short, there was a lack of leadership. No one could establish the consensus, so necessary and so much desired. René Coty, president of the Republic, faced a difficult task, all the greater in that his authority was largely symbolic. The reins of power were held by the leader of the government, the Chair of the Council of Ministers, who had been elected by a majority in the National Assembly. Not one party then held a majority. Furthermore, it was evident that neither the leaders of the principal political groupings nor the most influential individuals were likely to form a government because of rivalries, internal dissention, and ideological differences.

The situation was almost that of 1946, when de Gaulle offered his resignation. These divisions prevented the formation of a Cabinet of national union. Furthermore, the offices and the interests of the parties handicapped matters in several sectors. President Coty could not call on any of the "Great Four"—Pierre Mendès France, Guy Mollet, Antoine Pinay, or Georges Bidault—to form a government. There followed four weeks of consultations and discussions with the "Great Four" and various party leaders. The chosen leader was Pierre Pflimlin, the head of the MRP (*Mouvement républicain populaire*). He accepted President Coty's invitation. However, Pflimlin quickly encountered serious opposition from certain parties and several individuals who had been put forth for ministerial portfolios. He managed to resolve these challenges—a miracle that few observers had expected—and to constitute a government. He summoned the National Assembly for the afternoon of Tuesday, May 13, 1958, to be confirmed in office. This task proved complicated in the hemisphere of the Palais Bourbon (seat of the National Assembly) in Paris, and, as might have been expected, in the far-distant streets of Oran and Algiers (the White City). Those places were marked by a dangerous uneasiness, mixed with the thought of rebellion.

Algerians of all tendencies had long been wondering about the future of their relations of Metropolitan France. The status quo? Autonomy? Integration? Independence? Who could tell? Many of the Algerians whose language was Arabic or Amazigh were waging a war for independence. This war combined guerilla operations in towns and ambushes in the countryside, while the *Pieds-noirs* fought to maintain control of the territory as an integral part of France. Besides the war between the FLN and the government, conflicts were taking shape between the Metropolis and the provinces, between the government and the army, in which most of the higher-ranking officers were wedded to the idea of a French Algeria.

The fateful day of May 13 arrived. The crisis reached its paroxysm. The news of a government led by Pflimlin brought fear to the hearts of the Algerians of European origin. They were spreading alarm about the appointed government, calling it the "government of abandonment." The out-going Minister for Algerian Affairs, Robert Lacoste, had been called to resign from the Socialist Party over the cause of French Algeria, and he was given the unflattering sobriquet of *baudruche dégonflée* (a deflated bladder, once used as a balloon). Passions were rising and a fever seized the people. They sought a savior. The Gaullist antennas that had been set up some time before in the country went into operation (de Gaulle had certainly slammed the door in 1946, but he had not given up thoughts of power).

Certain pre-eminent members of the Algerian press were former Pétainists (i.e., collaborators, which implied working with the enemy, with the Vichy régime under the Nazis during World War II); nevertheless, the press called upon General Charles de Gaulle, who had also worked with Pétain, and even admired him before condemning him. Various patriotic associations united to establish a Committee of Vigilance. In an urgent appeal, this Committee called on the French people in Algeria to consider themselves organized against the establishment of a "government of abandonment," and they demanded that Pflimlin step aside in favor of a government for national salvation.

A general strike was proclaimed across the main towns of Algeria. Crowds assembled in the town squares in the afternoon. This was truly a human tide united by a single cause: to keep Algeria in the bosom of France by any means. It was a crowd of right-wing extremists, of "ultras," as they were called. Soon, ebullience spread through these groups. Dressed in T-shirts and canvas pants, the youth began to march while chanting, "Here's to French Algeria! Here's to de Gaulle!" under the eyes of the soldiers, who favored their cause, and the CRS who were responsible for maintaining order. Drivers, for their part, echoed the same noises through three sharp honks on their horns. Together, all these people were offering homage to the memory of the three soldiers who had been sentenced to death by the FLN. The demonstrators sacked the American Cultural Center. The leaders, who included many students, occupied the Government House and established a Committee to Save the Nation, with the blessing of the army.

The mob carried the day against the legal authorities very swiftly in Algeria. Unexpectedly, the rioters invested General Jacques Massu with the presidency of the "Committee to Save the Nation." General Raoul Salan, the commander in chief of the armed forces, also called the "the man who sold off the Empire," because of his defeat in Vietnam, found himself razzed by the crowds. Dressed in a parachutist's camouflage and a red beret, General Massu appeared on the balcony of the Government House. After tumultuous ovations, he demanded a government to save the nation under the presidency of General de Gaulle to resolve the crisis. In Paris, that news exploded like an artillery shell, and the Gaullist sensors went to work.

At almost the same moment, in the Palais Bourbon, Pflimlin was requesting the approval of his government. He encountered obstinate reservations. The approval was in no way certain. The discussion shed little light on the program intended by his administration. Some representatives—who might have been considered staff-members of the headquarters of the Right wing—made no secret of their disapproval. They insinuated that there was a need for a strong man and a strong government to match the brewing crisis. The atmosphere in the Palais Bourbon was as distraught as it was in the hinterlands far from the capital.

Throughout many towns in France, on that springtime day, the people were in a state of alarm. Many veterans, some in dress uniforms and others in combat gear, paraded to demonstrate their resolve, placing bouquets at the monuments of the dead. Imitating the demonstrators in Algiers, they also declared their trust in the "Man of June 18, 1940"—the date of de Gaulle's radio address from London, proclaiming Free France— then living in solitude in Colombey-les-Deux-églises. Clearly, General de Gaulle—the giant, the rebellious patriot who had spoken from London—captured the imagination of the French. At that time, how might one question the idea that he was the "living symbol of hope for France," as he described himself?

Messages were sent to the members of Parliament from every part of the country, demanding that de Gaulle establish a government for national salvation. In the churches, people prayed for national unity, and against the cowardice of the politicians. Nevertheless, student groups, labor unions, and other cells linked to the extreme left began to mobilize against a military putsch and seditious cabals. The time was dire, and the path leading toward civil war was wide open. Without question, these events involved the colonies in sub-Saharan Africa and in the overseas territories. Following the Second World War, there had been many changes. The French, like the British, somehow echoing President F. D. Roosevelt's Four Freedom call of 1941, sought anew to adjust their colonial regimes to the new post-war context. For France, the constitution of 1946 replaced the French empire with the French Union, and including the people of the "overseas territories," established a union based on an equality of rights and duties. It also disavowed the infamous legal system applied to the "natives," and ensured equal access to public office.

Franklin D. Roosevelt, Winston Churchill, Charles de Gaulle, and Henri Giraud at Casablanca conference, ca. 1943.

Going further, the constitution provided some representation of Africans in the Metropolitan assemblies of the Fourth Republic, that were the Parliament, or National Assembly, seated in the Palais Bourbon, the Council of the Republic, or Senate, seated in the Palais du Luxembourg, and the Council of the Union, seated in Versailles. This reform made the overseas people French citizens. Of course, the system for representation was far distant from democratic standards, and as well, the elected representatives of the colonies were not numerous enough, nor united in the Assemblies, to make any great difference. Nevertheless, through their links with the Metropolitan groups or by their direct alliance with some parties, they could exert some influence.

Thus, Africans were becoming familiar with the arcane operations of partisan politics in the Fourth Republic, and the effects even seemed to strengthen their role in the parliamentary game during the assemblies. Thus, it was not unusual to see one or two Africans included in the different governments that succeeded each other, especially after 1955. The *députés* (representatives), and particularly those of the large interterritorial movement known as the African Democratic Rally (*Rassem-*

blement démocratique africain: RDA), seemed to favor Pflimlin and his appointed government. The elected representatives of the RDA hailed the participation of their leader, Félix Houphouët-Boigny, the *député* from Côte d'Ivoire, as a Minister of State. Pflimlin went further and promised to revise the Title VIII of the constitution, to allow Africans further progress toward complete management of their internal affairs. Such a revision was fully in line with the necessities of politics throughout most of the overseas territories after 1957, when a programmatic law or fundamental law (a law applying to the legal system) called the Defferre Law came into effect; this law had introduced a certain degree of autonomy.

For the RDA—and especially after its third convention in Bamako, in September 1957—only a revision of the laws to this effect would strengthen the trust of Africans and "weld Africa and France in a common destiny." Sékou Touré, the master labor-leader of Guinea, his teammate, Saïfoulaye Diallo, and, from a party of opposition, Diawadou Barry represented the colony of Guinea in the National Assembly. Despite their silence, they observed the debate over adoption with the appearance of relief at the thought that the ministerial crisis would finally be resolved, but also with a feeling of worry about the events of that extraordinary day in the annals of the government.

Under such conditions, the African representatives—all involved in local projects within their territories—were not happy with the news from Algeria. The entire National Assembly, amid its debates, was forced to pay attention to the threats coming from the other side of the Mediterranean. Many speakers rose to condemn mob-rule and sedition and to oppose the idea of a government imposed from outside. For indeed, ever since the 18 *Brumaire* of Napoleon Bonaparte (the *coup d'état* of 1799), the army had succeeded in remaining loyal, despite the political crises. A *coup d'état*, it was stated, was alien to the French political tradition. Finally, late in the night, Pflimlim snatched a confirmation, thanks to a vote that was hardly convincing. His government was doomed to failure, for his majority vote fell short of the total of opposing votes and abstentions.

The new Chairman of the Council attempted to face the crisis. On May 14, he confirmed the appointment of General Salan to his position as Commander in Chief of the troops, although the latter had stated, unequivocally, his support for the idea of a government of national salvation. In the meantime, General Ely, Director of the Headquarters of the Army, resigned. President Coty appealed to the troops in Algeria not to create divisions. Still, tensions were rising within the army; communications with Algeria were cut off. Everyone expected a break, a forceful seizure at any moment.

Facing these events, on May 15, the hermit of Colombey was thinking of all the barriers that might impede his course of action: i.e., his age (he was 67), the gaps in his knowledge, limitations to his mental and physical abilities, and most particularly, the inconstant loyalties of the French people.[1] However, his passion for France was an imperative drive, or even his life's goal. Therefore, he declared that he stood ready to take over the powers of the Republic. The deterioration in national affairs quickly swayed hope and power in favor of General de Gaulle. Although a soldier, he had long been known for his attachment to a certain democratic and republican idea of the state, and that principle was much more reassuring than the militant bluster coming from the parachutist commanders in Algiers. However, immediate, direct action was required for the path forward was littered with traps and unforeseeable dangers. The situation was quickly deteriorating. In Algiers, General Salan was assuming all authority and working the Committee for Public Safety. Together, they controlled Algeria. In Paris, the reconstructed government obtained a "Critical State" status for three months, while the unions were issuing a call for strikes. Did the army still support the government? The question was open.

Those in a position to know did not think so. In this situation, many individuals—the former president, Vincent Auriol, the vice-president of the Council, the socialist leader Guy Mollet, Georges Bidault, Antoine Pinay, and including such persons as Pflimlin—visited Colombey, or wrote to him, extending a hand to the somewhat "enigmatic hermit." They were all aligned with the idea of a Gaullist government. None, in short, were ready to accept damage to the state, and tolerate its general dislocation. For de Gaulle and his men, the time had come to act. But how? It was no longer the situation he had faced on June 18, 1940, in London, when he spoke over the airwaves of the BBC. De Gaulle had no access to radio—private or public. They needed to find other means.

---

1. Charles de Gaulle, *Mémoires d'espoir*, vol. 1 (Paris : Plon, 1970), 23.

Fortunately, the media offered many paths to them. Who could doubt the power of writing in a highly literate nation, or that of the immediate audio-visual impressions transmitted by journalists in pursuit of great events?

The press, in print or electronic form, was becoming more and more of a global enterprise and promised to become an enormous power that was hard to control. De Gaulle knew this. He was skilled in the art of communication and in encounters with journalists, and he would exploit that talent. He called a press conference in the Palais d'Orsay, not far from his office in Paris, on Rue Solférino, for Monday May 19, to become publicly involved. On this occasion, the national and international press would find him in the splendor of his age: somewhat older and heavier, of course, but fit and alert, *ingambe* (spry), as he would say. The hermit of Colombey returned, incognito, to Paris, not without regrets at the sight of armored cars and police barricades placed on the principal arteries and around the public buildings. According to the reports by Jean Lacouture, it was the most massive mobilization of police forces ever put forth in Paris. Journalists had to make their way through a triple barrier of the armed CRS.[2] De Gaulle was serene before the imposing cohort of the national and foreign press. A major American television channel was covering the press conference, live and unabridged.

All over the world, "the man" aroused undeniable interest; his press conference counted as a major event of the day. Speaking in a spirit respectful of the law—by temperament he was a jurist and a historian— he sketched out the cause of the crisis, the substance of his succinct statement made on May 15, and then, as a dialectician, he stated that the crisis might be "the start of a sort of resurrection." And the journalists' impression? It was favorable. The Enigmatic man of Colombey had managed "to dominate, without crushing, to convince rather than to defeat."[3] In short, he sounded reassuring.

Events tailed handsomely and swiftly, while history followed its imperturbable course. The crisis became ever more urgent, as was confirmed by the news of May 24. Paratroopers from Algiers joined the units stationed in Corsica and took over the provincial government. They set up

2. Jean Lacouture, *De Gaulle*, vol. 2 (Paris: Seuil, 1985), 470.
3. Lacouture, *De Gaulle*, 471. See also *Le Monde*, May 20, 1958.

Committees of Public Safety, to "give an example to the Metropolis." The reinforcements sent from Marseilles allowed themselves to be disarmed. Detachments of paratroopers even landed on the French mainland. This attempt at a *coup d'état* could not be overlooked. In Paris, everything was in disarray. An order was given for a general strike and for civil resistance. On May 26, de Gaulle met Pflimlim and asked him to resign, to avoid bloodshed and other undesirable consequences of a civil war. As though to demonstrate his authority, he issued a public declaration on May 27 in which he required that the military forces should cease all operations and allow civil authority the task of determining the necessary regular process, which meant his return to leadership over French affairs. It was no surprise that the army obeyed. De Gaulle's return to power was assured.

Still, the government and the Parliament continued to prevaricate. This was normal and foreseeable, as the events would lead to their removal from decision making, along with the end of many individual careers. However, facts had to be faced: the government had no power. On the afternoon of May 28, spreading from the Place de la Nation to the Place de la République in Paris, an enormous demonstration to "Defend the Republic" took place: hundreds of thousands of demonstrators followed Mendès France, François Mitterand, Edouard Daladier, a former head of the government, Hamani Diori, *député* from Niger and vice-president of the Assembly, and Waldeck-Rochet of the Communist Party. They were chanting, "Put de Gaulle in a museum!" They could not stop the course of events, however. Pflimlin delivered the resignation of his administration to President René Coty. Before offering any official statement, Coty arranged an interview between de Gaulle and the Chair of the Council of the Republic, Gaston Monnerville, from the Antilles, and the Chair of the National Assembly, André Le Troquer. These notables managed to agree upon the forms for the transition of power. Monnerville was won over to the idea but suggested there should be a limit of six months, at maximum, for the special power. That evening, de Gaulle was admitted to the Palais de l'Élysée in a highly emotional atmosphere, and the decision was made.

On May 29, in an official message to the Assemblies, President Coty announced his decision to call upon the "most illustrious Frenchman" to form a new government, and to resign should the effort fail. This was a most surprising declaration from a politician known for deliberative thought. Marshal Juin—a former classmate of de Gaulle at St. Cyr, the French military academy—announced that the army would "follow de Gaulle to a man." Given this situation, most of the barons of the régime acquiesced. De Gaulle accepted the charge to establish a government, to make use of full powers for a period of six months, and to prepare and submit a new constitution through a referendum. Thus, the bets were placed. France and Africa faced the prospect of a new era.

On Sunday, June 1, in a spirit that respected legal formalities, de Gaulle appeared in the Palais-Bourbon, seat of the National Assembly. As Raymond Barrillon, who witnessed the events, reported in *Le Monde*: "The *Hemi-cycle* was packed, and the galleries into which the public had struggled to find seats were absolutely crowded. Timid and somewhat disconcerted, the General slipped up to the bench of the government. With quick glances to right and left, he gauged this Assembly. He walked up to the rostrum. From the extreme right and the extreme left, an imposing silence. Returning to a house that he had never loved, where he had never felt at ease, and which he had been forced to leave, the appointed President of the Council hastened to deliver his message."[4] In rhythmic and emotional speech, General de Gaulle "resumed the situation" and "showed what he expected" of the Assembly: Full powers, the mission to offer a new constitution to the nation, and the suspension of the action of the Assemblies. Then he withdrew, and the debates began.

How did the African members of the *Chambre des députés* perceive de Gaulle? Most of them did not know him at all. Their experience, in the Assembly or in the Council of the Republic, took place in a context from which Gaullism (as a structured political movement) had been absent for years. In general, they only had impressions or vague feelings. Their image of the General was mixed up with the image of the Enigmatic hermit of Colombey, about whom people talked much and whom many feared in the political circles of the Metropolis. However, for a great majority of the inhabitants of French Africa, "the man of June 18, 1940" was better known as "the man of Brazzaville": the legendary French leader who, in a speech given in Brazzaville in 1944, for the first time in the annals of colonization, had mentioned the idea of having "Africans participate in the

---

4. See *Le Monde*, No. 4155, June 3, 1958, pp. 44-5.

management of their own affairs in their territory."[5] People perceived him as an "anti-colonialist colonialist."

The elected representatives from overseas territories understood that the constitution of the Fourth Republic—whatever its great weaknesses and enormous obstacles to effectiveness— reflected the commitments made during the Conference of Brazzaville at the start of February 1944. This system, grounded in a liberal tendency, offered to the colonized a means of participation and a voice in French politics that was not insignificant. Thus, the overseas representatives had some influence in Paris. The factitious behavior in Algiers disturbed them deeply. They were faithful to the constitution. They were faced with a dilemma. How might they reconcile their respect for legal forms and their respect for de Gaulle (who had presided in Brazzaville), and more specifically, his rise to power under the threat of a *pronunciamiento*, an illegal *coup de force*?

Thus, it was not surprising that on May 13, many of the Africans aligned with the left condemned the threat of insurrection or of a military *coup de force* by Massu and Salan. Bit by bit, however, the fears of the African politicians diminished as events began to favor General de Gaulle. In certain circles, people suggested that these developments might serve the interests of Africa. As confirmation of these suppositions, many influential Gaullists (including many former colonial Administrators) approached African members of the Assembly to remind them that the General was an anti-colonialist, and of his vision of Franco-African relations. It was not easy to achieve unanimity. Many *députés* based their decision on considerations that were, at times, of a personal nature, or at others, partisan, depending upon their party and their position in the semi-circular chamber. On that date, however—June 1, 1958—party discipline was giving way to some extent to the impulses of individual consciences. The *députés* and the Senators gave little weight to the acerbic criticisms mounted by the black students, connected with the UNEF, the activist organization of the Union of the Students of France, against the

---

5. From September 1941 to June 1943, Brazzaville was both the capital of the French empire and of the French Resistance. De Gaulle chaired a conference there, starting on January 30, 1944, with the goal of redefining French colonial doctrine. Since that time, de Gaulle has been known as the "Man of Brazzaville," because he supported the idea of having Africans progressively involved in political affairs.

General, or the support he received from the Generals, the factions, and the ultras of Algiers.

The group of African members of the Parliament could be divided into two camps: on one side, the Pragmatists determined to be on the side of the winners, and on the other, the "Wait-and-See" group, who wished to learn more about the intentions of the man who had been nominated as President of the Council. Among the Pragmatists, one could count the *députés* Houphouët-Boigny, Modibo Kéita, Fily Dabo Cissoko, and for them de Gaulle's anti-colonialism was an historic fact of great political importance, and one that should sway all other considerations, including the somewhat less than legitimate conditions of his return to power. They felt that Africa should trust the General and join the movement that was bringing him back to head the government of the Republic in Paris.

This position was easiest to understand on the part of Félix Houphouët Boigny, *député* for the Côte d'Ivoire and President of the RDA. His connections with de Gaulle at that time went back some six years. The two men had begun to take the measure of each other in March 1953, during a sweeping tour that brought the General back to Black Africa. In Abidjan, he was welcomed with honor and pomp by Houphouët and his party. Appreciative of this courtesy, de Gaulle, in turn, often welcomed Houphouët to his office on the *rue Solférino* in Paris.

Thus, following the events of May 13, the Minister Houphouët-Boigny quickly sided with de Gaulle, realizing that the General was the only possible arbiter, and the only ensurance for republican institutions. "In fact," he said, "I immediately foresaw a change in the fate of our overseas territories. I was quickly convinced that the spirit and the hopes of the Fundamental Law would be followed, and perhaps even exceeded by the Gaullist dynamic."[6] Moreover, some Gaullists from the General's entourage, such as Roland Pré, former Governor of Guinea, suggested to Houphouët that he should continue his ministerial portfolio under the new government. The *député* from Côte d'Ivoire did not hesitate. "He appeared at the side of the General and sought plain dealings with him in everything." Therefore, the pragmatists voted for the investiture. They had great hopes.

---

6. Quoted in Gabriel Lisette, *Le combat du RDA* (Paris: Présence africaine, 1983), 329.

As for the "Wait-and-See" group: they were not intrinsically hostile to de Gaulle, but they had serious concerns about the modalities of his return to power. They were, for the most part, politicians of intellectual and legalist temperament. For such *députés* as Ouezzin Coulibaly and Nazi Boni of Upper Volta (now Burkina Faso), Lamine Guèye, Mamadou Dia, and Léopold Sédar Senghor of Senegal, Diawandou Barry, Saïfoulaye Diallo, and Sékou Touré of Guinea, the appointment of General de Gaulle under the current conditions posed a problem of constitutional principles. In their opinion, there was a contradiction between the re-establishment of republican order and the imposition of a government by factional elements. The dichotomy disturbed them.

The "Wait-and-See" group saw in the investiture of the new government the undertones of a *coup d'état*, despite all appearances and despite their admiration for de Gaulle. Their point of view was even shared by former Gaullists. As Raymond Aron so nicely put it, "*C'était la séduction après la sédition*" (It was seduction after sedition). This meant, to some extent, that "formally, de Gaulle returned to power legitimately; it was not he himself, but others who had performed the *coup d'état*."[7] The Assembly was faced with an ultimatum, and, therefore, gave a legal veneer to a *coup d'état*.

The situation troubled the Africans of the "Wait-and-See" camp. In the account of Mamba Sano, a former *député* from Guinea, such considerations explain, in part, why Senghor hesitated to answer an invitation to join the government. Bernard Cornut-Gentille, former Governor General of French West Africa in Dakar, and at that time, in 1958, the nominee as Minister for Overseas France, along with Georges Pompidou, a former classmate of Senghor and Chief of Cabinet for General de Gaulle, quickly invited this *député* to accept their proposal. What might have become of the Federal Executive, if this Senegalese *député*, known for his attachment to that institution, had participated in the government?

Because of Senghor's hesitation, and since Houphouët was then chosen, de Gaulle refused any thought of a compounded solution, in which he would have brought into his government the leaders of both principal African political movements: Houphouët-Boigny's party, the RDA (*Rassemblement démocratique africain*), and the PRA (Party or African

---

7. Raymond Aron, *Le spectateur engagé* (Paris: Julliard, 1981), 209.

Alliance), of which Léopold Sédar Senghor was one of the leaders. Senghor would, however, take a seat on the Constitutional Committee, an appointment that reflected both his connections and his known abilities as an interpreter of constitutional texts.

Sékou Touré, of an activist and leftist disposition, had some difficulty in accepting the imbroglio that defurled in May-June of 1958. Furthermore, despite his good relations with Cornut-Gentille, he did not possess the assets of Houphouët or Hamani Diori, the Vice President of the Assembly, and he found himself on the sidelines. Thus, he preferred to wait before offering a definite opinion. The same was true of his fellow-partisan, Saïfoulaye Diallo, and their opponent, Diawandou Barry, who sided with the party of Mendès-France. In short, the "Wait-and-See" group found it hard to accept the revolt of the armed forces and the extremist colonials in Algiers. However, they knew that the Fourth Republic suffered from a deep weakness, and that even its supporters found it difficult to believe it would survive. They abstained. They did not wish to sanction illegality, nor to hinder the march of history.

During the debates, François Mitterand, Pierre Mendès France, and other speakers made an impression by their consistent argument and their stinging attacks against personal power and an "investment extorted by the threat of sedition." De Gaulle felt such statements as malevolent, specifically those of Mendès-France and Jacques Duclos, the communist leader, although he had some regard for these men. However, the General had come out as the victor in two different definitions of patriotism and democracy, and so, in consolation, he described such statements as "the last spasms" of the dying Fourth Republic. Indeed, he noted, "All had been settled. Only details remained."[8] At the end of the debates, the investiture of the new government was approved by a majority of 329-224 votes. This marked the end of a long period of political surprises and uncertainties. A new era was about to start. As de Gaulle would comment, what was coming was "undoubtedly a deep transformation, not a revolution. The Republic was being renewed but was still the Republic."[9]

How can we explain those days and those events? France was perturbed in all her parts in May of 1958, and the events gave birth to a

8. De Gaulle, *Mémoires d'espoir*, 32.
9. De Gaulle, *Mémoires d'espoir*, 32.

new political regime—this is the origin of the Fifth Republic. An answer offered by Jean Lacouture has some relevance. In the opinion of this far-sighted observer, the Fourth Republic disappeared "without striking a blow, but not in a suicidal mood; the political order did not yield to the blows of the military but collapsed before a combination of threats and pressures. De Gaulle's return was not due to the tanks of Massu; he came through a regular—or almost so—process."[10] As Mendès France so aptly put it, "There was no *coup d'état*, because the Parliament lay down."[11] Facing a *fait accompli*, the French in the homeland and overseas acquiesced.

Late in the evening of June 1, Sékou Touré returned to the studio in the cul-de-sac of la Verrerie, in the third *arrondissement* of Paris. It belonged to Fodéba Kéita, who had established the dance troupe, the *Ballets africains*, and since 1957, had been a political leader of the town of Siguiri in Guinea. He was somewhat tired, thoughtful, and taciturn. His thoughts ranged over the current events, the distant past, France, and Africa for great events had just unfolded in which he had had no part. That thought gnawed at him because of his own view of himself and of his sense of responsibility. However, the Algerian uprising and the inevitability of actions leading to the liberation of the colonized peoples affected him.

Touré had no sympathy for the cause of the Ultras—they were the symbol of the nationalism of the oppressors. Touré was pleased that the struggle in Algeria had set in course the beginnings of political change in Paris, and even across France. He was, however, and to some extent, content in the Parliament. The dissolution of the Fourth Republic, a system that he knew how to maneuver in a marvelous manner, affected him with uncertain feelings. It was vanishing without any signs of the future order. What might that presage for Africa? For the RDA and his native Guinea? These were questions to which he had no answers. And melancholy became overwhelming! Slowly, sleep came to him.

---

10. Lacouture, *De Gaulle*, 487.
11. Pierre Mendès France: "Je ne voterai pas sous la menace de l'insurrection et du coup de force militaire" (I shall not vote when faced with the threat of insurrection or a military *coup de force*). *Le Monde*, June 3, 1958, p. 4.

CHAPTER 2
SÉKOU TOURÉ IS EXCLUDED FROM THE CONSULTATIVE CONSTITUTIONAL COMMITTEE

T HE INVESTITURE OF the government on June 1, while a unique and important event, offered no grounds to the new President of the Council of Ministers for celebration. Time was short, and it was not the moment for congratulations. Reflection and stern action were required. For de Gaulle, the investiture marked one of the preliminary steps toward his great plan to endow France with efficient and coherent political institutions, and to set her firmly on a path toward renewal that to him, seemed the true condition of her future fruition. In the short term, the need was to provide means of action consonant with the republican traditions, but still with effective legislation. Thus, on June 2, the new head of the government had the National Assembly vote, as an emergency, a bill concerning full powers within the French territory, and another on special powers for Algeria—the cradle of his authority, that also carried the risk of becoming its tomb, given the persistent anarchy in civil administration and in the armed forces.

There was still the framework to be erected for the new construction, meaning the assemblage without which the renewal would lose all substance. This was the project for revision of the constitutional law, the source of the endemic scourge within the Fourth Republic, and thus, the keystone in any proposed reforms. Given the importance of the matter, a two-thirds majority was required. On June 3, the Assembly was called to approve laws on this project. To the General's surprise, no sooner was the session opened than the *députés* gave signs of a new vitality. Apparently, they were recovering from the torpor induced by the events of the recent weeks, and so offered a last, and impressive, spectacle of the habitual practices of their semi-circular chamber. Thus, as a witness recalled, "the debates got mired down, mixed up, and transformed into a festival of confusing amendments."[1]

And so, Olivier Guichard, a faithful Gaullist, alerted his "master," the President-elect of the Council. De Gaulle decided to come to the National Assembly to restore order and to save the proposed legislation. He appeared relaxed and affable. His demeanor was quite different from that he displayed on the day of the investiture, as people observed. Good-humored but determined, he participated in the debates, answered the speakers, and clarified issues. Clearly, he was playing a game of seduction. And the Assembly, as Raymond Barillon wrote, was "caught by the charm and hypnotized."[2] Acting as an astute psychologist, full of irony, and as a leader concerned with decorum and due process, the new master of France, as he wrote in his memoirs, attended this "supreme" session "so as to swathe with good will the last moments of the last Assembly of the regime" of the Fourth Republic.[3] Deep down, he was delighted that he could now build that which the circumstances of the immediate post-war period had prevented.

These proprieties led to a result beyond hope: the proposed law was adopted by a vote of 350 to 161. In turn, the Senate, or Council of the Republic, gave its approval. These impressive and unexpected votes were the sign of the emergence of a national consensus that the representatives, whatever their many differences, felt bound to respect. The French were fed up. They wanted to turn a page and move on. Jean Lacouture, noting this, commented, "The Fourth Republic entered its tomb without much entreaty. The sound of some soldiers' boots, some superficial negotiations and underhand manipulations, a distant clap of thunder, and out of the blue the appearance of a sovereign talent armed with little more than his certainties—the god, of the machine, as he himself wrote, preferring that term to that of machination."[4] For de Gaulle it was a great victory, and one that was personal.

---

1. See *Le Monde*, June 4, 1958.
2. Raymond Barrillon, *Le Monde*, June 4, 1958.
3. De Gaulle, *Mémoires d'espoir*, 34.
4. Lacouture, *De Gaulle*, 502.

That vote gave de Gaulle a free hand. Henceforth, he could apply himself to the task of reconstruction. In the analysis of Sylvain Soriba Camara, the June 3 law delegated to the government the mission of drawing up the draft of a new constitution that would organize authority in France and the relations with French territories overseas, in accordance with precise directives.[5] First, the government had to collect the opinions of a Consultative Committee, composed of members appointed by decree and of members of the Parliament named by the relevant commissions of the Assembly and of the Council of the Republic. Second, the proposed legislation had to pass through the Council of Ministers. Finally, following opinions expressed by the Council of the State, the proposal had to be submitted to a referendum before it was adopted.

Thus, the development of the constitution passed through several stages, starting with the draft of a proposal by the government, discussion of this document by the constitutional Consultative Committee, passage of a final version by the government, and then the submission of this last stage to the peoples of France and the overseas territories. Given the principal requirements of this proposed legislation, two capital elements imposed themselves: 1) the urgency of passing the law, and 2) the predominant role of the government in drawing up the new constitutional document. In contrast to the experience of 1945, which gave rise to all the problems of the constitution of 1946, now the government, and, therefore, its leader, started all the discussions that should lead to the draft proposal. He drew up the document and received opinions from the consultative bodies and finished the procedure and the drafts. Thus, one might note that he was the first source of all, that everything passed before him, and that everything came back to the one who had initiated it. Therefore, we feel that being a member of the government, and particularly a Minister of State, had capital importance. Such a minister with access to everything—such a minister could contribute to the debates, he could offer suggestions or introduce suitable amendments, and then follow them through on all levels.

On this point, the role of the Consultative Constitutional Committee, while very significant, was nevertheless that of consultation and not

---

5. Sylvain Soriba Camara, *La Guinée sans la France* (Paris: Presses de la Fondation nationale des Sciences politiques, 1976), 78.

of decision-making. Obviously, the Committee disposed of great resources, including the power to demand that the government answer its questions and observe its opinions (those of the counselors). All told, however, that the government had the final word. We stress this point to show how the opinions of the only minister of African origin—Felix Houphouët, as it happened—prevailed in the end. To a great extent, the debate over urgent issues, such as the system of the federations of French West Africa (AOF: *Afrique occidentale française*) and French Equatorial Africa (AEF: *Afrique équatoriale française*) and of the federal executive offices that were of most importance to Africans, should be seen in the light of, and through the opinions and influence of, Houphouët. He was the man of the hour for African affairs.

In that year of 1958, in fact, the different parts of Africa were wondering about their right to independence, and more specifically, what would be the rules governing territories in this process. In the past two years, two contrary positions had emerged: on the one hand, there were those partisans who viewed independence in the context of the existing ensembles of the territories; on the other hand, there were those who viewed independence from the narrow perspective of individual territories. The two groups were not marked by their silence. The question of participation in the bodies appointed to draw up the new constitution also attracted considerable interest. Within those bodies, directives were discussed and formalized.

The varying perspectives of the participants on these constitutional assizes would etiolate the direction of the discussion, and to some extent, the outcome. Hence, the political considerations that weighed in the selection of the thirty-six members of the Consultative Constitutional Committee were of great importance. Political allegiance, personal rivalries or alliances influenced the choice. De Gaulle alone, by the strength of his will and by the precise direction of his program, along with the appointment of his cabinet, kept the bodies charged with consultation and decisions free of the taint that characterized the usual practices of the Fourth Republic. The primary qualification at this point was membership in the circles close to the General.

And in this labyrinth of intrigues, what were people saying about the Guinean *députés*? Were they part of the "Gaullist cells"? Were they marked to take on important positions in the government or in the Consultative Constitutional Committee? The dean of the Guineans in the Assembly in 1958 was Diawadou Barry, representing the BAG (*Bloc africain de Guinée*: African Alliance of Guinea). He had held his seat since 1954, when he defeated Sékou Touré in the special election organized to replace Yacine Diallo, who had died. Barry was linked to the Radical-Socialist party of Pierre Mendès France, and he was noted for his gravity and his composed demeanor. He was deliberative in his statements, but he was not known for being a Gaullist. Moreover, had not Mendès criticized the return of the General? Had he not been one of the leaders of the great anti-Gaullist march in May at the Place de la République? The Radical Socialist party was opposed to the new government. Moreover, back in Guinea, his party, the BAG, stood out as an inter-ethnic national coalition of the major leaders (and as such, it continued to lose ground everywhere to the party of Sékou Touré and Saïfoulaye Diallo). In contrast to most of the French organizations, the Radical-Socialist party, with which Barry was affiliated, voted against the investment of de Gaulle's government. Therefore, Barry had no seat on the Constitutional Committee.

The two other *députés*, Sékou Touré and his companion on the electoral slate, Saïfoulaye Diallo, had been elected as representatives of the RDA, and so, like all the others elected on that slate, they were linked with the UDSR (*Union démocratique socialiste de la Résistance* [The Democratic Socialist Union of the Resistance]), led by François Mitterand. It was admittedly a small party, but it carried great weight. This point explains why, in 1956, Mamadou Konaté, former *député* of the Soudan (Mali), was elected Vice President of the National Assembly, and after his death in 1957, Hamani Diori, *député* from Niger, assumed the same office, as well as the participation of other RDA members of Parliament in the several governments of the Fourth Republic. Sékou Touré and Saïfoulaye Diallo, elected in 1956, and notwithstanding their reputations as important organizers and public speakers, still lacked experience within the confines of the Parliament.

Despite this obvious disadvantage, Sékou Touré benefited from a good public image. He was known as an engaging person, and for his activities in the labor movement, his contributions to the debates on matters of social law, and for his intelligence, activism, and energetic and heartfelt drive. He was considered the figurehead of the left wing of the RDA. He had already gained distinction as a leader of decisive quality, as an impassioned and enthralling advocate for the people. He was also seen as a leader who sought fame and power; this was the opinion of the observers, in September of 1957, when the RDA held a convention in Bamako. There, he triumphantly carried propositions in favor of maintaining the Federations of West and Equatorial Africa. His aureole seemed to over-shadow the "old" wing of the RDA leadership. Sékou Touré's growing nimbus destined him, as they thought, to become a member of the Con-stitutional Consultative Committee, to represent the views of the signif-icant African left. How would the leaders of the party react to such a situation?

It was a difficult question. Houphouët, as an African knowledgeable and respectful of certain traditional values, considered Sékou almost as a younger brother, one whom he knew to be hot-headed and rash. Let us explain. Since the 1920s, there had been many Guinean and Soudanese (Malian) Muslim families, speaking Maninka, in Côte d'Ivoire. They were engaged in transportation and commerce in all its forms, and especially in the local trade, following the harvest of fruits and grains that moved those commodities. They were known as Dyula, because of their profes-sion (in Maninka, *dyula* means trader). They enjoyed cordial and frater-nal relationships with the indigenous communities of the forest among whom they lived. Some of the first members of the RDA came from these Dyula, as can be seen in the case of al-Hajji Lansana Kaba of Bobo-Dioulasso (at the time, part of the colony of Côte d'Ivoire), who was the honorary President of the RDA until his death in 1956.[6] The center of the movement was in the *cercle* (district) of Bouaké, that incorporated Yamas-soukro, where Houphouët was born and the seat of his chiefdom.

In Bouaké, Mamadou Touré, nicknamed *Petit Touré* (little Touré), a member of the family, introduced Sékou Touré, his cousin and a young labor-leader, to the *député* Houphouët. We might stress that Mamadou was the grandson of the legendary Kémé Bouréma, younger brother of Samory Touré and a commander in his armies. (On this topic, we should also note that the young members of the Touré family in Kankan and Sanankoro, in the district of Upper Guinea, quickly adopted Sékou Touré as one of theirs; in fact, his father came from the present Republic of Mali,

---

6. Collected by the author in 1955, during a stay in Bobo-Dioulasso, and later confirmed in 1969 by additional research.

while his mother was a descendent of the Samorian line). Through sustained material assistance, that provided critical help during the difficult periods of the PDG, Houphouët, the rich planter and *député* from Côte d'Ivoire, proved his respect for his "younger brother" in Guinea. Eye-witnesses to the struggles of the PDG in the districts of Upper Guinea and Forest Guinea could still, in 1980, remember the visits and the material support that came from Côte d'Ivoire, specifically through the good offices of the *député* Ouezzin Coulibaly and other supporters of the cause.

The exceptionally close relations of these two men, in addition to the organizational and militating abilities of the PDG cells, contributed, in part, to the establishment of the RDA in the territory of Guinea and to its later success. This was considered a given fact, as Ibrahima Kaké emphasized in his work on Sékou Touré.[7] In Guinea, the PDG received aid from the PDCI (Democratic Party of Côte d'Ivoire) from 1951 to 1956. However, despite their "brotherhood" and their membership in the same party, the two personalities of Sékou Touré and of Felix Houphouët were in opposition. Houphouët-Boigny was impressive, through his small stature, his pondered eloquence, and his exceptional pragmatism. Sékou Touré, of average size, was equally impressive for his elegance, his fiery language, his dynamism, and his ardent idealism. How could these two temperaments paddle the same pirogue? In June of 1958, the RDA and the Consultative Committee in Paris faced this question.

De Gaulle established his government. Houphouët became a Minister of State. The composition of the Cabinet reflected the urgencies facing the General and the times. He brought together representatives of the parties that had voted for his appointment, along with the principal functionaries of the State and the Gaullist faithful. Sékou Touré fulfilled none of these conditions, and so found no place in the government. Still, as was foreseen by Bernard Cornut-Gentille, Minister for Overseas France, and even Michel Debré, the Guardian of the Seals, Touré's abilities could have entitled him to a seat in the Constitutional Consultative Committee, whose 36 members—observing the laws passed on June 3—were to be, in part, elected by the Parliament and, in part, appointed in secrecy. Sékou Touré, however, was followed by controversy. This was a feature of his nature.

---

7. Ibrahima Baba Kaké, *Sékou Touré: le héros et le tyran* (Paris: J. A. livres, 1987), 41.

Bernard Cornut-Gentille, former High Commissioner of the Republic in Dakar (Senegal) followed the career of Sékou Touré from the early 1950s on. He recalled how the young Guinean first committed himself to the cause of the CGT (*Confédération générale des travailleurs*: General Confederation of Workers), a union supported by the Communist Party, and then established the UGTAN (*Union générale des travailleurs d'Afrique noire*: General Union of African Workers) to advance the independence of the African labor movement. The former Governor General was aware, of course, how this bold leader of the masses succeeded in a few years in expanding his tiny party into the principal political body in Guinea. Such achievements were to be praised.

Sékou Touré arriving at the airport in Slovenia

In the eyes of Cornut-Gentille, Touré embodied the prototype of the leader that "we should have with us, and not against us." He had an acerbic tongue; he sowed trouble. He was feared. Putting him on the Constitutional Consultative Committee might neutralize the African far left. For these reasons, the Minister for Overseas France did not hide his desire to see the RDA advance the candidacy of Sékou Touré among the twenty-six members to be elected by the Assembly. The Minister Houphouët-Boigny, the "older brother" of Sékou Touré, did not see things in this way; he knew his colt. Other members of the RDA in the Parliament reportedly sought the same post. The stakes were significant. Houphouët wanted no surprises. Perhaps he still remembered that in 1957, at the third convention of the RDA in Bamako, he had been placed in the minority, in part, because of Sékou Touré. Therefore, fearing the changeable character of his impulsive and rebellious junior, he hoped for a more trustworthy voice, who would remain in agreement with his political views and never deflect from them. Thus, his choice went to Gabriel Lisette, the eloquent *député* from Chad; he was born in the Antilles and served as vice-president of the RDA. The selection was a defeat for the Minister Cornut-Gentille, but he did not reproach himself after the fact.

There remained thirteen members of the Constitutional Consultative Committee to be appointed, pursuant to the law passed on June 3. These members were not required to be members of Parliament; they were chosen according to their qualifications (there was, still, an exception: that of the *député* Paul Reynaud, who would chair the sessions). True to his beliefs, Cornut-Gentille put forth the name of Sékou Touré to de Gaulle to be member of the committee, by his dual qualifications as a member of Parliament and as the leader of the largest African labor union. De Gaulle found himself perplexed.

Georges Chaffard offers an account of the discussion between the President of the Council and his Minister for Overseas France, as follows:

> *"So, Cornut-Gentille, isn't it for Africans themselves choose their men?"*
>
> *"Just so, My General, but…"*
>
> *"But, Cornut-Gentille, since Houphouët himself states that the presence of Sékou Touré is not necessary, and he vouches for that fact, what more do you need? Houphouët knows his business."*

However, the former High-Commissioner, very well-informed in the facts about Africa, did not admit defeat. He went to see Michel Debré, the Guardian of the Seals, who oversaw constitutional revisions. Debré agreed. However, de Gaulle maintained the position taken by Houphouët. Sékou Touré was, therefore, excluded.

Here, some commentary is required. At that critical time, the man from Côte d'Ivoire was the only African, in the close entourage of General de Gaulle, holding the status of Minister of State, and hence, *ex officio* a member of the Constitutional Consultative Committee. The doors of the Hôtel Matignon, home to the offices and the residence of the President of the Council, were open to him. This strategic position gilded his image and reinforced his influence at a time when his star was beginning to fade in many African lands, because he opposed the Federations of the AOF and the AEF and the Federal Executive. When the convention in Bamako in 1957 required him to take a position on the right to independence, he spoke out in defense of the right of each territory to govern itself and to establish its relations with the Metropolis directly.

This position was directly opposed to the proposition of a Federal Executive power in Dakar and led to a breach at the core of his movement. From 1957 on, the unity of the RDA was in many regards only a semblance. The principal ideas that had led to the unity were now being shattered. All over, arguments against African confederations were spreading among the influential classes. However, the commitment of Guinea to the principle of a unified West Africa, under some federal system, was well known, and Houphouët was aware of it. However, in Paris, Houphouët's influence permitted him to ensure the success of his opinions. On the banks of the Seine, he won what he lost on the banks of the Niger in Bamako.

And so, during that summer of 1958, Paris became the prime battleground among the different streams of African politics and nationalism. The Minister of State was not mistaken, and I. B. Kaké was correct in stressing the point.[8] Fortunately for Houphouët, de Gaulle listened to him in the matters concerning overseas territories and trusted him. His attitude reflected a certain form of liberalism that was engaging and paternalistic, while perhaps also "racialist." Such points help to explain why Sékou Touré was set aside; he was the fervent champion of the cause of uniting the colonial territories in a federal structure. This was a crucially important issue that the Ivoirian *député* settled as he chose.

Given the urgency of restoring the authority of the State and to ensure the proper relations among institutions, de Gaulle took a decisive step. He charged Michel Debré, the Keeper of the Seals, and his limited cabinet with the task of drawing up the plans to propose a new constitution.

---

8. Kaké, *op. cit.*, 87.

On June 19, 1958, the draft was offered for comments. After long reflection on the question, de Gaulle himself became actively involved in the process. He wished to ensure that the project would agree with the plan he had proposed on June 16, 1946; among the Gaullists, the plan was known as the Bayeux Program, looking back to the time when, in that city of Normandy, he had set forth his clear and definite vision of a constitutional plan for the post-war government, before he departed for the United States.

In summary, that speech/vision, considered by many as the fundamental speech in political Gaullism, "blamed the country's problems on instability and disorder, and demanded new institutions to create a balanced and strong state." Without any equivocation, the visitor in Bayeux declared that "executive power must derive from the head of state; it would be his task to reconcile the public interest in the choice of personnel with the tendencies present in Parliament; his was the duty to name the ministers, first of which was the prime minister who would direct the policies and the work of the government." Underlining the relevance of that speech, de Gaulle wrote, in his *Mémoires d'espoir*, "Living now in Matignon, topical issues assail me ... But while dealing with them, I direct the work of reforming institutions. Twelve years ago, I identified and published the critical issues involved. What we shall accomplish is, all told, what has been labeled the "constitution of Bayeux," because it was there that on June 16, 1946, I outlined what was needed for France."[9] A consolidation of executive power, and the election of the President of the Republic through universal suffrage were some of the elements of that "constitution" that served as a model.

At the working sessions, one would encounter, besides the General, Houphouët-Boigny, Guy Mollet, Pierre Pflimlin, and Georges Pompidou, all of them faithful to the democratic-republican idea. As for Michel Debré, Keeper of the Seals, he worked in his office on Place Vendôme with a team of experts on matters constitutional and juridical, along with representatives from the Ministers of State. In mid-July, the two groups compared their work and adopted a draft that was called the "Red Notebook" from the color of the cover. This document succeeded in reconciling a parliamentary and a presidential regime, stipulating that the

---

9. De Gaulle, *Mémoire d'espoir*, 34.

Executive was supreme, and putting the responsibility for government upon the Assembly. The president granted himself the power to call a referendum and to dissolve the Assembly. These points differed greatly from the former practices of the Fourth Republic that aimed at reducing the prerogatives of the Executive Branch and submitting it to the whims and caprices of the Legislative Branch. The draft was submitted to the Constitutional Consultative Committee, and their work started on July 29 in the Palais-Royal.

As might have been expected, de Gaulle sat in on meetings of the Committee several times to hear the suggestions and to clarify his thoughts. He knew that Africa expected much from him. Among the thirty-six members of the Committee, besides Minister Houphouët, we can identify four African members of Parliament: Léopold Senghor and Lamine Guéye from Senegal, Philibet Tsiranana from Madagascar, and Gabriel Lisette from Chad. They were particularly concerned with the relations between France and the overseas territories. What did the draft have to say about this very specific question?

The document stipulated explicitly: "The Republic offers to the populations of the overseas territories who demonstrate the desire to participate in it new institutions established on the common ideals of Liberty, Equality, and Fraternity." The text mentioned a new political entity called a "Federation" that was nothing other than the direct association of the Territories with France. To become members of the "Federation," the Territories might retain their status, indirectly, as parts of the territorial collectivities, such as the units known as *Afrique occidentale française* (AOF, French West Africa) or *Afrique équatoriale française* (AEF, French Equatorial Africa), or they might freely and directly join the "Federation" following deliberations and decisions from their territorial assemblies.

The draft agreed with an important Gaullist idea, i.e., the need to form a structured whole, different, of course, from the *Union française* (French Union) that was too rigid and too colonial, but dominated by the French president, while still ensuring autonomy (if not yet independence) to the old colonies. This reform would portray France as a power engaged in a policy of amicable decolonization, and in world affairs, this image would be positive. The Franco-African federalism that would be termed the community was nevertheless somewhat different from the African federalism based on the continuation of the AOF or the AEF; as the PRA and Sékou Touré argued for the latter and Houphouët rejected it, there inevitably followed opposition and confusion. De Gaulle thought well of Africa, and in his own manner, respected Africans. He left it to them, however, to decide upon their choice, since his own mission was to work on France. In service to that goal, if required, he would become the apostle for a certain form of decolonization, and he would shape France as he intended, not worrying about the Africans.

In hindsight, the draft of the constitution, as laid out, did not answer the aspirations of most Africans during that summer of 1958. Why didn't Senghor and Lamine Guéye defend continuance of the Federation more vigorously? They didn't speak up too strongly! Why? Their country, Senegal, was the principal beneficiary of the Federation of West Africa. Furthermore, the draft, so far, made no mention of the principle of a "Right to Independence," demanded by the students, the labor unions, the PRA, and even some factions of the RDA. The idea of this right and the honor of having inscribed it, despite his hesitations, would go to Houphouët, as he himself recounted it at the 40TH anniversary of the establishment of the RDA in 1986, at Yamassoukro.

The text of the draft allowed territories to withdraw from existing Federal institutions. For many Africans, the proposed text was an invitation to division or Balkanization, a term that had become pejorative. Moreover, the draft made no mention of the existence of functional federal entities, such as the Great Councils of the AOF and the AEF. In short, the proposed reforms addressed the weaknesses in France but failed to address any number of matters relating to Black Africa (this was due to the cleverness of Houphouët and, of course, to the disagreements among the African members of Parliament).

In most African political circles, the first reports on the draft project were met with disappointment and concern. And de Gaulle's speech, delivered over the radio to the people in the overseas territories on July 14, 1958 (Bastille Day, and the French national holiday), exacerbated these feelings, less because of his lyrical effusions than because of the lack of specificity.[10] Apparently, Paris did not understand that in tropical Africa, "History was speeding up" at that very time.

---

10. See de Gaulle, "Allocution radiodiffusée le 13 juillet 1958" in *Discours et messages: Avec le renouveau, mai 1958-juillet 1962* (Paris: Plon, 1970), 24-25.

To illustrate this point: during the 4ᵀᴴ Convention of the PDG, held in Conakry on June 5-8, Sékou Touré clearly stated his preference for the creation of a great African state that, when independent, might establish a commonwealth with France. He noted further that the "liberal concessions and other gestures of good will" from the Metropolis lagged behind the maturity of Africans, and hardly matched their aspirations. The Convention hoped that the constitutional revision at work in Paris would lead to the recognition of a right to internal autonomy, to the establishment of a federal executive branch, and to the transformation of the *Grand Conseil* (Great Council) of the AOF into a Federal Executive. Later, on July 28, when the special session of the Territorial Assembly opened, Sékou Touré offered the following remarks: "General de Gaulle wishes to unite the French nation, and this is a noble undertaking to the benefit of France and the peoples associated with her. Why should we not include and facilitate the role of political movements that also want to create, in Africa, an African nation? The solidarity of France and Africa is inconceivable without the unity of the AOF and the AEF."[11]

As a second example, the convention of the PRA was held in Cotonou (Dahomey, now Benin), July 25-27; the PRA was, second to the RDA, the largest inter-African political grouping. The delegates, coming from all over save from Côte d'Ivoire, included celebrities such as Lamine Guèye, Léopold Senghor, and Mamdou Dia from Senegal, Nazi Boni from Upper Volta (now Burkina Faso), Bakari Djibo from Niger, Fily Dabo Cissoko and Hammadoun Dicko from the Soudan (Mali), and Diawadou Barry from Guinea. They all demanded: "First, independence. The rest to follow." In its "bottom-line" program, the PRA demanded that the draft of the constitutional project should include a right to independence and to a federation of territories, such as were active in the AOF and the AEF. How might one disregard this political effervescence in favor of federalism and independence, on terms quite different from those in the project being prepared in Paris? It was around such issues that the true battle over the Federal Executives was conducted.

Let us return to Paris, to the Palais-Royal. It was the seat of the Constitutional Consultative Committee. They set up a working-group for

---

11. Sékou Touré, *L'expérience guinéenne et l'unité africaine* (Paris: Présence africaine, 1959), 66.

overseas territories. When it came to the articles concerning the African colonies, as one might have expected, two positions emerged that it would be hard to reconcile, each offering interesting arguments sustained by a notable of substance who enjoyed the support of influential French allies. On the one hand, there was Senghor, with a degree in grammar, celebrated for his incisive analyses of legal texts. His mandate was to present not his own perspective, that was somewhat moderate, but that of the PRA, which stressed immediate independence, a unification of the territories, continuation of an independent federal system in Dakar and in Brazzaville, associated with France through bonds of confederation.

The second proposition, which almost matched the draft of the constitutional proposal, reflected the perspective of Houphouët-Boigny. While he was the President of the RDA, he had not yet obtained the consent of the Policy Committee in his party; nevertheless, and obviously, he still had great influence. Houphouët had long found the federal institutions clumsy and burdensome; he had doubts about their worth. In his view, these institutions interfered in the relations of each territory with the Metropole, and, unfortunately, demanded financial support. This meant that the rich territories bore the load of the federal capital of Dakar, and of the federal bureaucracy. He felt that those funds could and should be employed in ways more useful to the development of those same rich territories. Thus, debates over the federal executive branch involved economic and egoistic dimensions, and also most certainly Malthusian elements. Houphouët never made the statement explicit, but everyone knew that his land, Côte d'Ivoire, was the richest territory of the AOF. Therefore, many observers believed that the hostility of the Ivoirian leaders toward the federal executive was directed to preventing their country from becoming the "cash-cow" of the AOF. During that summer of 1958, Minister Houphouët did not conceal his opposition to the notion of Federal Exective branches in Dakar and in Brazzaville, and to any Franco-African association that would not observe the principle of direct cooperative connections between Paris and the territories.

Houphouët did not reject the question of independence; he was an African nationalist and the President of the RDA. Independence was the logical conclusion to the great liberation movements of the colonized peoples, whose goals had driven the RDA from its creation. In 1957, in Bamako, in the presence of numerous notable French persons, including

Mendès France and François Mitterrand, Houphouët spoke in support of recognizing a "Right to Independence" of African countries, and of the establishment of a federal community with France? His words were certainly framed by the circumstances. Thus, his struggle in the Interministerial Committee to have that right recognized was to be expected, as well as his eventual appeal to de Gaulle to have it written into the constitution. However, the federal community with France was not, in its conception, the Federal Executive with a capital in Dakar or Brazzaville.

In 1958, Minister Houphouët believed that "the immediate independence demanded by the PRA was premature and would not serve the major interests of French-speaking Africa." Ghana, the eastern neighbor of Côte d'Ivoire, had become independent from Great Britain in 1957. Its example seemed to offer some indicators of the cost of independence. He sought to warn his Francophone colleagues against the temptation of cutting the umbilical cord with France, the "generous donor." We should note that in the time since the presentation of the Draft Project, new elements had arisen pertinent to these, specifically African issues. Gabriel Lisette proposed a principle of self-determination for the territories, while the ideas advanced by Senghor received more and more attention. The suggestion was made that the status of a territory might be reviewed after its first choice, and even that there should be a review every five years.

This is to say that the Constitutional Consultative Committee split in a way that recalled the Fourth Republic. Friendships, alliances, and influences played their part. At first, the discussions served the proposals of the PRA, thanks to the analysis offered by Senghor and to the skills of Lamine Guèye, Dean of the SFIO (Socialist Party) in Africa. Therefore, many French leaders, of diverse orientations, respected for their opinions, and including, among others, Pflimlin and Paul Coste-Floret of the MRP and Guy Mollet of the SFIO, counted among the camp in favor of territorial unities and a Franco-African confederation to be reviewed every five years.

Houphouët was tenacious and did not give an inch. In the Constitutional Committee, he defended his proposal with vigor. His attachment to a federal Franco-African Community that could endure, without the constraints of federalism, impressed a good part of the members of the Committee, and specifically, de Gaulle. Houphouët counted on him, the "Strong Man" of France, the one responsible for the idea of a constitutional revision. Houphouët paid a visit to Matignon. He laid out his thoughts methodically. His argument against a federal executive, and especially against the idea of reviewing Franco-African relations every five years convinced de Gaulle; his belief in simple, solid, and enduring constructions was legendary. Henceforth, there would be no doubts, the two statesmen agreed. The overseas territories were called to choose either the *Communauté fédérale franco-africaine* (Federal Franco-African Community), with all its benefits, or else for "Immediate Independence," without France, and with all its consequences. The choice was clear, and everyone knew what was involved.

Certain of support from above on the part of the master of Matignon, Houphouët now turned to his own Africa to put his household in order. The stakes in the game demanded such action. To strengthen his position and to demonstrate his control over his movement, he convened a meeting of the RDA Coordination Committee in Paris for August 3RD. He could allow himself such a move because without exception, all the principal leaders knew in their hearts that they owed him something. In this meeting of capital importance, he could count on Ouezzin Coulibaly, his long-standing friend; Coulibaly was a *député* for Upper Volta (Burkina Faso), and the political secretary respected by both the right and left wings of the party and known for his skills as an orator and as a mediator. Coulibaly issued a plea to preserve the unity and solidarity of the party. In the end, his argument carried the day, despite reservations from the sections from Guinea, the Soudan (Mali), and Senegal.

They adopted a program that agreed with the proposal of the President of the RDA: autonomy of territories, elimination of the Governor Generalship in Dakar and Brazzaville, and refusal of a new Federal Executive. This meant the individual evolution of each territory toward independence, and direct bilateral relations with Paris, but also international cooperation in areas of shared interests. This plan, apparently, was not enough for the Ivoirian leader. He felt they had to banish all equivocation and show a common front before the authorities in Paris.

They then decided to dispatch a delegation to present the RDA proposal to General de Gaulle. They felt that this mission was the duty of Sékou Touré, both because of and despite the reservations he felt about the proposal. However, the rule of democratic centralism, that demanded respect for majority decision, won out and took force. During the special audience with General de Gaulle, on August 5, the *député* from Guinea performed his mission honorably. There was joy in the leadership of the RDA. De Gaulle and Touré had met and talked. All the obstacles had been flattened. To all appearances, there was cohesion and agreement. A tip of the hat to Houphoët-Boigny: he had pulled off a "coup of coups" with the General and with Sékou, two personalities with different temperaments, if not also different natures. Houphouët, deep down, congratulated himself and rejoiced. There were no longer any doubts about his abilities as a leader, a strategist, or a diplomat because he knew how to apply himself patiently, await the right moment, and then gain his goal without striking a blow.

As for Sékou Touré, he was pondering. It wasn't easy, he told himself. Had this mission to meet the General been entrusted to him to assuage his sensibilities? Or was it to trap and weaken him? How might he reconcile the proposal put forth to de Gaulle with the proposal that had been offered earlier, on July 28, at the Territorial Assembly in Guinea and in Cotonou. The pill he had swallowed left, for a long time, a bitter taste, and he was not about to forget it quickly. His bile began to act up and his ire to overflow. For a change of atmosphere, he decided to travel quickly to Dakar to attend the meeting of UGTAN (*Union générale des travailleurs d'Afrique noire*: General Labor Union of Black Africa), the central labor union, over the constitutional question and the referendum.

On August 6, a hot summer day in which Paris seemed emptied of its usual crowds and suffered from sweltering heat, Sékou Touré stayed late in his studio apartment. He received visitors and made phone calls to Paris and to Africa. That afternoon dressed elegantly in a fine custommade suit, he went out about his business. Then, as usual, he took his coffee and had dinner with his friends. That night, Touré made a visit to the Keur Samba, a select cabaret-dance-hall on the Left Bank, not far from St. Germain des Prés, thronged by the youthful African elite and a Parisian clientele in search of "typical dances" marked by hot and bewitching Afro-Cuban rhythms. Unlike many Africans in France and elsewhere, he never touched alcohol. Among his favorite distractions, he enjoyed dancing and checkers (in Africa, generally called *damier* from the name of the board). Touré excelled in the syncopated steps of the cha-cha-cha and the meringue, as well as in the languorous dances of the bolero and the tango. It was a delightful evening, and he enjoyed himself. The next day, he took flight for Dakar.

In the meantime, the debate between the two perspectives was moving to a paroxysm in the Constitutional Consultative Committee. On August 8, de Gaulle felt impelled to attend, to arbitrate, or rather to impose his point of view. Houphouët-Boigny counted among the very few "in good odor." In the afternoon of a day of enfeebling heat, de Gaulle and his suite entered the great hall of the Palais-Royal to encounter a body of nervous constitutional counselors. After the meeting had opened, he addressed the question relating to the overlapping of political authorities. Then de Gaulle raised the issue of Franco-African relations.

Everyone who heard him was amazed at his arrogant, self-important language, that was threatening and blunt. As S. S. Camara reported, de Gaulle expressed his point of view in a manner so forthright that he alienated the African observers.[12] You may judge the tone from the report of Jean Lacoututure: "Why fight over abstract words such as 'federation'? That is not the true question; it lies in the opinion dividing association and secession. Truly, we hold together, or we divide. We must establish a structure. The government decides to call it a 'Federation'.... Federation, confederation—these are only words. I, myself, may say 'Confederate.' But we will not force anyone to join. There shall be no question of a status granted or imposed, for the territories shall be free to choose their status when the referendum is held. Should the territories say 'No,' there follows secession, and they shall face the risks and dangers of this hard world in which the imperative is towards unity. And should secession carry the day, the Metropolis will fulfill all its consequences." "People may wish for secession. That path entails tasks. It involved dangers. Independence has its costs. The Referendum will show whether the idea of secession wins out. But we cannot imagine an independent territory and a France that continues to assist it. The government will understand the consequences made evident though the demonstration of such a decision. An affirmative answer, however, would be refusal of secession...."[13]

This was a time when television had yet to be known in Africa—from Niamey on the Niger to the new city of Nouakchott in Mauritania. At 8

---

12. Camara, *La Guinée sans la France*, 85.
13. Lacouture, *De Gaulle*, 572

P.M., the leading classes in Africa tuned their radios to Radio-Dakar, the station of the Federation of the AOF, or Radio-Brazzaville for the AEF, to hear the news from the Metropole. In Conakry—as usual, in the rainy season, swamped by heavy rains—Diawadou Barry, a *député* and Karim Bangoura, advisor to the *Union française*, and other leaders of the BAG were listening at the home of Framoï Bérété, the president of their party that had become the Guinean chapter of the PRA.

They had faced many disappointing moments. From 1956 on, the PDG was favored by the colonial authorities; the Governor, J. Mauberna, was complicit in such actions. Still, they offered no criticism of France or its actions toward its colonies. However, the statements they heard that evening left them perplexed. Throughout his long career in political activism, Framoï—the man with white hairs in his ears—could not recall any speech showing such intransigence delivered by the Metropolitan authorities, and still less on the part of the legendary "Man of Brazzaville."

Diawandou Barry, for his part, foresaw vaguely that the President of the French Council would give short shrift to the arguments of the PRA, presented to the convention in Cotonou in May, that favored immediate independence and a Federal Executive branch. And Karim Bangoura, who had earlier displayed his talent as a diplomat and his skills in business negotiation, felt that one had to wait for the results of the Consultative Constitutional Committee, and the publication of the final law. They all shared the same opinions: de Gaulle was a tactical genius, but authoritarian and ill-disposed to opposition. And so, they preferred to wait and learn what the reaction of Sékou Touré, their adversary, might be.

Sékou Touré's reaction came swiftly. On August 9, in firm tones during an interview on the air-waves of Radio-Dakar, he made no secret of his disappointment with the General's statements. He found them shocking, outrageous even, ballasted with inappropriate and extortionary threats. "Hearing General de Gaulle yesterday," he answered a journalist, "frankly, I was shocked. We were told that we might take independence, but that there would be consequences. Well, my reply, for my part, is that those consequences might not only be African. They might also be French."

Touré felt offended, and his reaction was even more virulent in that it was the natural conclusion to the internal doubts that had been gnawing at him since August 5, and his audience with de Gaulle on the part of the RDA. The latest statement of the head of the French government was truly a surprise to him, and challenged Africa and Africans, and—why not?—might offer an unexpected opportunity. And so, he called upon a sense of honor and of "African dignity," words that became true leitmotifs in his thought and speech, and that symbolized pride and courage. He was, no doubt, showing the idealism expected from his youth.

At any rate, because Touré was aware of the history of his family and of Guinea, of the glorious pages in African history of the 19TH century, and specifically, the resistance, the leader of Conakry treasured the "Africa of proud warriors" and the builders of empire whose epic should inspire the current generation. His self-image as an African, and his responsibilities as a leader, forced him at that time into profound reflection. Extremely thin-skinned, did he succeed in overcoming that trait? However, his vision went far beyond the narrow frame of his natal Guinea. He was an activist who wanted to become the voice of the deepest Africa, the Africa of the peoples, a continent that deserved respect and should cultivate a sense of unity. De Gaulle apparently was ignorant of the depth of these feelings. Therein, no doubt, lay the hornets' nest that might ignite a conflict, a tragedy.

On August 14, the Constitutional Consultative Committee completed its work. In the place of the term "federation," it chose that of "community," a word suggested by Tsiranana. The Committee also accepted two important amendments. The first allowed any territory that might have voted "yes" on the referendum to achieve independence later, without secession from France and thus, with the guarantee of French assistance. The second related to the unity of the territories forming the federations of *Afrique occidentale française* and *Afrique équatoriale française* (French West Africa and French Equatorial Africa), but in its text, did not mandate such institutions. It allowed for the entry of the territories into the community, as a group should they so wish; but these terms did not quite match the principles of a Federal Executive. It was a compromise. General de Gaulle secretly agreed to these two amendments and had planned to announce them at his mass rally in Brazzaville, a city with historic resonance in the Gaullist world, where he hoped the announcement would have an explosive effect.

Politics seems to go together with spectacle, as we can see through literature and through history. The various committees established following the events of May 13, 1958, completed their assignments. The

Assembly accepted the draft constitution. The government promised to present this draft to the peoples of France, in the homeland and overseas, within a period of five weeks. And so, de Gaulle prepared for the referendum and in France, and for his trip to Africa. That voyage would prove decisive in many matters, especially in Guinea.

CHAPTER 3

TRAVELS IN AFRICA AND THE SPEECH IN CONAKRY, AUGUST 25

T HE DATE IS Monday, August 25, 1958. For almost six days, General de Gaulle, head of the new French government, has been travelling with his suite across Africa, down to Madagascar, so that he, as a sign of respect, might present his plan for the reform of the constitution to the peoples of the overseas territories, and to request, in person, their approval. He hoped that the approval would be overwhelming. The colonies had been living under the law known as Loi-cadre or Loi Gaston Defferre for some twenty months. This law established internal autonomy within the territories, under the control of a government led by the leader of the dominant party. However, still, by law, the Colonial Governor held certain important powers.

The thought behind this governmental law was to prepare the colonies to manage their own affairs, and hence, to prepare Africans for the functions of administrative duties. However, the great challenge was to reconcile this process with the Federal institutions of Dakar (capital of the *Afrique occidentale française*, AOF: French West Africa) and Brazzaville (capital of the *Afrique équatoriale française*, AEF: French Equatorial Africa), that enveloped all the colonial territories as members. The exceptions were Togo and Cameroon, former German colonies; following World War I, they were governed as mandates from the League of Nations (and later, the United Nations). This was the institutional situation when de Gaulle undertook his periplus of 1958—and how different it was from the tour he made in 1953 as an ordinary French citizen!

Everywhere, the General's visit aroused—for the moment—euphoria in the capitals. It was the occasion for grandiose festivals and folkloric dances. His welcome was warm and triumphal. When he stopped in Fort-

Lamy (now N'Djamena) in Chad, people recalled with pride and with feeling the name of Félix Éboué, a Governor of the AEF native to the French Antilles, who during World War II, was the first to commit his territory to the government of the Free French under de Gaulle. They also recalled the beginning of the epic deeds of General Leclerc, who contributed to the liberation of North Africa in that war. It was, in short, a summary of the significant contribution made by Africa to the war effort and to the liberation of France.

In Tananarive (Antanararivo), Madagascar, the first real stop on this periplus, the General and his following were impressed by the jubilance of the people. The guest of honor made an important speech before the Representative Assembly, and declared, "We shall offer all imaginable possibilities. The bills presented to the peoples of the overseas territories will not exclude any solution, including secession." On that great island, bathed in the blood of martyrs to anti-colonial resistance and the national uprising of 1947, the speech elicited mostly favorable responses at the Assembly and among the crowd on the street. Yet, in certain circles, some wondered why de Gaulle avoided pronouncing the word "independence," and why he talked of "secession," an equivocal term. Many felt that this ran against any idea of a true community of free peoples. In Tananarive, though, de Gaulle, with a gesture full of theatricality, revived the general delight by pointing his finger at the Queen's Palace on the mountain, and announcing that, "Tomorrow, Madagascar will be a new state, such as you were when the Palace of your kings was inhabited."[1] This constituted a formal recognition of a right to independence. And with good cause, Tsiranana, President of the Territorial Council, exulted in the thought of leading his country to sovereignty.

The next day, the officials left Madagascar with fanfare. The presidential jet took a majestic west turn and crossed the immense canal of Mozambique that separates the island from the African continent; from the windows, the travelers could easily contemplate the green dense forest that covers the huge Congo basin extending from the east in the Indian Ocean to the Atlantic. De Gaulle and his convoy admired the forest, the waterfalls, and the vast grasslands that make the magic of this amazing environment. After some four hours of flight over the tropical forest, the

---

1. De Gaulle, *op. cit.*, 37.

convoy arrived at Brazzaville, the cradle of Gaullism in tropical Africa, on August 23. Charles de Gaulle recalls history, part of his own, decades ago. He felt like a pilgrim, and proud of the effect of the message he had delivered there in January 1944. And, now, in 1958, a leader, he saluted the political effervescence that was shaking Africa. Here, at his second stop, the joy of the throngs reached its peak. The crowd was delirious. In that historic site, many memories came to the mind of the great traveler. He evoked them by going to bow before the stela erected in memory of Felix Éboué, who had been Governor General of the AEF during World War II. This was also a great opportunity for the General, a specialist in history and in peoples, to further burnish the glory of his "pilgrimage." He transformed himself to an apostle "spreading the good word" of decolonization and agreement among the nations, while pronouncing for the first time, the long-awaited word "independence."

Without ambiguity, de Gaulle acknowledged that Africans had a right to independence. He put it in these terms: "It is natural and legitimate that African peoples should reach the political level on which it will be their task to govern themselves." As he saw it, this became possible within the context of the new Community that he was proposing. He withheld the key word from those who were saying, "We have a right to independence." "Most certainly, yes," continued the orator. "Furthermore, anyone who might want it may take it immediately. The Metropole is not opposed. But should the electoral body of the African territories vote 'yes' on the Referendum of September 28, this would mean that by free determination, the citizens have chosen to establish the Community. And again, within this Community, should some territory... feel, after the passage of time, that it was capable of facing all the challenges of independence, well! It should then decide through its elected Assembly. Thereafter, the Community would act, and an agreement would settle the conditions of transfer between the territory moving into independence and the Community itself. I guarantee, in advance, that in this case again the Metropolis will offer no opposition."[2]

This unexpected speech aroused enthusiasm in the audience even more because most of the members of the local elite, like those in Côte d'Ivoire, were favorable to the notion of the association of the territories

---

2. Quoted in Lacouture, *De Gaulle, op. cit.*, 576.

with France, rather than continuance of the current Federal system. The speech reinforced the position of leaders who were known for their hostility to immediate independence. Thus, it had the effect of a bomb, exploding under the equatorial skies of Brazzaville on the bank of the mighty Congo. The speech defused, to some extent, the thesis of the extremist groups. The effect was exactly what the General had expected. The speech resolved one of the fundamental themes in Franco-African frictions. "After such a speech, there were no more problems. The great Franco-African debates had reached a solution." This was the opinion of Gabriel d'Arboussier, a strategist and the Secretary General of the RDA, and President of the Great Council of the AOF in Dakar. Who might vote against such a bill?

Here, de Gaulle displayed a measure of moderation, compared to the uncompromising speech made on August 8 before the Constitutional Consultative Committee in Paris. The tone of the speech delivered in Brazzaville was far less shocking, even though the orator stated that the "Metropole also, within the Community, would retain her own free authority and might, should she judge it necessary, break the links with one or another territory." In this point, de Gaulle displayed some familiarity with the ultra-conservative propositions of Raymond Cartier, the editor of *Paris-Match*, a very popular magazine. Those ideas were full of political and cultural short-sightedness, very close to xenophobia and racism. The General did not cite this source, but the ideas were recognized in certain French circles, and the argument could be perceived as an undertone in the statements of some colonials. Africans were not blind to these undertones. These tinges had fueled discussions, specifically in the circles of the labor movement and among students who had been exposed to Marxist writings. All these ideas finally led to pressure upon the leaders, no matter what their ideological leanings.

Colonization seemed more and more to be interpreted as a business matter, and that now, it was facing a moment of final accounting. The idea was that to "be the net negative or positive, we must now move toward liquidation of the operations." However, not, of course, within the stock market that rules the capitalist system. Henceforth, the situation was reversed. Costs and duties were pushed back onto the colonized territories themselves, whose people and resources had, in the past, supported the profitability of the colonial enterprise. This was the new vision of colonization and decolonization, emerging in the class of leadership, and that Raymond Cartier was pleased to spread among the French middle classes in the Metropolis and in the colonies, alike. The speech in Brazzaville was meaningful on another level. By establishing a reciprocal bond between the colonies' right to independence and the right to separation from the Metropolis, de Gaulle showed that the process of decolonization was not a one-way path, following only the wishes of the colonized. Thus, de Gaulle slipped in the notion that henceforth, the Metropolis—in a contrast with the 19TH century, during which European powers went to war for colonial expansion—might make do without the colonial system, and quite possibly, without any major economic or financial damage. Colonization, a matter of business, was no longer profitable, and seemed to be the point of view taken by de Gaulle.

The legitimacy of the right to independence of the colonies was balanced by the prerogative of the Metropolis to choose whether to cooperate with a given territory, and, in short, to abandon it if that seemed necessary. Mutual recognition of the right of each partner to act as they chose seemed a pledge of willingness to cooperate. Obviously, de Gaulle hoped that cooperation would come about to preserve the interests of France and Africa. This conviction, tinged with paternalism, made his speech in Brazzaville a great speech, and one that was very revealing of Gaullist policy toward the colonies. The approach was calculated to avoid the possibility of conflicts over liberation.

The argument presented in Brazzaville by the General seemed much less intransigent, and certainly much more diplomatic than the virulent and simplistic theses of Raymond Cartier, who felt that the economic requirements of the colonies would, henceforth, fail to balance their advantages. De Gaulle was an astute statesman and had no doubts about the many advantages that might come to France through her relations with Africa; but he also observed the strong and almost inevitable throbbing of nationalism. This most likely explains the change in tone between the speeches of Tananarive and Brazzaville. The General did not engage in anti-colonialism through spite, at that place beyond the Equator, even though deep down, he might have been contemplating the idea of unloading France's colonial hindrances and passing down in history as the man who abolished the colonies. He who—only three weeks earlier—refused with disdain any discussion of the processes leading to independence, and employed extortion, now accepted, for he was constrained by history, to make concessions in that vein. History seemed useful to him.

From Brazzaville, on Sunday, August 24, General de Gaulle and his suite travelled to Abidjan where they were awaited by the Minister of State, Houphouët-Boigny, in his fief. The event was huge and spectacular. As reported by Jean Lacouture, a special correspondent for *Le Monde*, the leading newspaper in Paris, "The enormous welcome demonstrated by the people of Abidjan on Sunday for the General de Gaulle was not only a homage to a representative of France, but also a true festival of community, liberty, and fraternity. It was also a successful master-stroke for the RDA, that large party of the masses, that proved able to mobilize an entire city that was eager to express its fervor by shouts of "Yes! Yes!" From the Mogo Naba, Emperor of the Mossi, who had made a special trip down from Ouagadougou in Upper Volta, to the *bana-bana* (itinerant peddler) of Treichville, the President of the RDA, with his friends, were literally throwing their people into the arms of the head of the French government. And up from this seething human mass, from this glistening whirlpool, there rose a joyous clamor of friendship."[3]

In a short speech, de Gaulle plainly stated that the moment of liberty was, at the same time, the moment of African responsibility. This idea, with its allusion to the costs of sovereignty, as we must recognize, conformed nicely with the line that Houphouët-Boigny, President of the RDA, and his Ivoirian team, had been following since the third Convention of their movement in Bamako in September 1957. At that time, with effort, they had succeeded in establishing the principle of federalism and of imperious cooperation with France. Houphouët found it impossible to imagine independence rationally without considering economic resources. This was a form of realism, attenuated, but still along the lines of Cartier, that became a permanent leit-motiv in the vision of the community, as conceived by the head of the French government and his African minister. The two statesmen understood each other.

The speech delivered in Brazzaville pleased the Ivoirian leaders who were known in the sub-region for their allegiance to the notion of independence at the territorial level. The speech helped to define and to reject

---

3. Jean Lacouture, "De Gaulle à Brazzaville," *Le Monde* No. 4225, August 24-25, 1958. See also No. 4225 for August 26, 1958.

the obstacles that "federal extremists" were raising against the unity of the RDA and the proposed Referendum. In the opinion of those leaders, the recognition of a right to independence, as proposed by the General, demolished the substance of the arguments offered by the left wing of the party against the divisive nature of the proposal. For one could vote "Yes!" without giving up liberty and sovereignty within the unity. Echoing with his Ivoirian host, General de Gaulle confirmed his commitment to "that Franco-African Community that will bring about many changes." The crowd—the women sporting cloths printed with the image of de Gaulle—was still delirious when the General and his following moved on to the airport, heading for Conakry, Guinea, barely two hours away by plane.

Given these enthusiastic welcomes, we may well wonder if the African peoples of the French colonies in AOF lived in the same world of nationalism and anti-colonialism that was shaking the Maghreb, Cameroon, and the Portuguese territories, where people were fighting to gain independence through armed struggle. In the AOF, by contrast, decolonization moved with friendship and fraternity. It was also proof that in the AOF under French domination, political awakening, even after years of simmering growth, retained a deliberate spirit. Houphouët, having rejected an alliance with the French Communist Party, sought to define himself as a man in the middle, quite different, of course, from the leaders Reuben Um Nyobé and Félix Moumié of the UPC (Union of the Peoples of Cameroon).

The nationalism of the AOF could be distinguished from that of the AEF (*Afrique équatoriale française*) by its gradual and non-confrontational character. The initial goal of the leaders of that region was not to sweep out colonialism and to build a new activist order in its place, but to adapt to the colonial regime, to modify it in part through institutional reforms, to create ever wider spaces for Africans. In short, people were accommodating to the colonial regime rather than rejecting it. In many regards, the laws proposed by de Gaulle were in harmony with this "gradualist" school of West African nationalism.

Blazoned with the Cross of Lorraine, the emblem of de Gaulle, the presidential plane took off from Port Bouët, the airport of Abidjan, in the early afternoon, and tore through the grey clouds that were piling up in the tropical skies in the season of the monsoon. The thick clouds concealed the palm-groves and other plantations that were the source of the economic prosperity of the colony. The plane rose and set its heading for Conakry. Swift and majestic, the great bird clove the air and rose above the peaks of the great Atlantic tropical forest. Over Liberia and then Sierra Leone—English-speaking lands—it flew. And soon, came the descent.

Through the round windows, the passengers could see a jade-colored ocean and a characteristic seashore. It was a fine and impressive spectacle, despite the threatening clouds that morning in the heart of the rainy season. A coast indented with rivulets spread before them, offering estuaries, low and swampy plains, meanders, a vegetation of mangroves and palm-trees, and many islets, all lying beneath the Kaloum escarpment to the east. The plane entered the "land of the southern rivers," the former name of the colony. Seen from above, Conakry displays a belt of coconut trees, straight and interlaced avenues, rectangular houses, and presents a magnificent appearance—a peninsula that was truly the pearl of that part of the Atlantic coast known as the Gulf of Guinea. And it was the entire territory of Guinea, not only the capital, Conakry, that welcomed de Gaulle, President of the Council of France.

Despite oppressive, hot, and humid weather, an ever-increasing throng, well-situated and organized, overwhelmed the Route du Niger of the city of Conakry, in the quarter of Gbessia where the airport was located. The law-enforcement officers, in fine uniforms, in great number, and nevertheless, very nervous, worried about the possible spontaneous reactions of this overjoyed human swell. Rich, varied, and loud music sounded out. The spectacle offered by the people was a mixed festival of colors and sounds, representing the four natural regions of Guinea. Jenbe and other drums, balafons, four-string guitars, koras and harps, lutes and cymbals accompanied the songs in local languages that the musicians delivered in honor of the party that "defeats evil, and remembering the past, sows well-being" (that phrase truly slips political considerations into the rejoicing of the people). The party in question was, of course, the party of Sily ("elephant," in Susu), symbol of the PDG of Sékou Touré. A group of two or three women—the dancers relieved each other—performed the rhythmic dances. Everyone seemed ordained by a distant and invisible hand.

Close to the airport, the military band was in place. Within the thronged hall of the airport, the crowd showed impressive obedience to their instructions, and all were in their assigned places. Representatives of the European community, civic dignitaries, along with religious leaders and the heads of the powerful local cells of the PDG (*Parti démocratique de Guinée*)—the regional branch of the RDA—had come in their best finery. Beyond them, in the VIP lounge, were Jean Mauberna, wearing the white uniform of the Governor, surrounded by his cabinet, Sékou Touré, in an immaculate robe and in his function as President of the Council of the territorial government, along with the members of his government and officials from the Territorial Assembly, and other dignitaries. They exchanged their thoughts amicably while looking up to the heavens.

The control tower announced that the Caravelle would land very shortly. The military band moved onto the tarmac, followed by the dignitaries. The plane landed, taxied to its space, and stopped. The gangway was rolled into place, and the doors of the airplane opened. And very soon, the General appeared in his khaki uniform, and the *képi* with its three gilded stars on his head. At the bottom of the stairs, the Governor and the President of the Council of the government waited. De Gaulle descended the stairway. There, the Cross of Lorraine and Sily the Elephant met. A military detachment offered the honors to the sound of "La Marseillaise." The General, the Governor, and the President of the Council then reviewed the assembled troops and made their way to the VIP lounge to the sound of the unrestrained acclamations of the crowd and the shouts of, "Long live de Gaulle!" and "Long live Sily!"

Spontaneously, a chorus of men and women sounded out a song exalting the hero:

> *You are at home here, you are in our city, your city.*
>
> *Your arrival today is not by chance; it carries the weight of fate.*
>
> *Our chief, give orders, give commands. Raise your head and behold this crowd.*
>
> *It is yours. It rises and sits down as you desire.*
>
> *This people is yours and we greet you.*

In response to a song addressed as much to the illustrious guest from

France as to the prodigious local leader, meaning Sékou Touré, the crowd applauded.

Perfect order was the rule, disturbed only by the clicking of the cameras of the European journalists. The General was impressed. The two leaders crossed the VIP lounge and graciously greeted the groups assembled outside. Then they took their places in the Chambord, a luxury Simca, an official car black as night, to the sound of music and the repeated cheers of the crowd. In turn, the dignitaries went to their own vehicles. And slowly, the cortege progressed toward the town.

On all sides, along the sidewalks, stood a polychrome crowd, wearing European-style shirts or African robes or African ensembles of a uniform color. The crowd sang, danced, laughed, and hailed, with loud cries, the passage of the two distinguished leaders standing in the car. At every crossroads, as though on a stage, there were performers: here you heard the voice of Malinké *jeliw* (griots) from Upper Guinea, there a chorus of Susu women, or else, the sad sound of the fiddles and the flutes of the Fula, or again, the mysterious drumming and the polyphonic sound of performers from the Forest Zone, with their masks and other relics. The folklore and the masks displayed the cultural diversity of the country. And all along the route, at various places, resounded the calls, majestically orchestrated, for independence.

For about an hour, a rich and harmonious polychrome ballet, obeying slow cadences, spread like a long python, majestic and interminable, along a route of some fifteen kilometers through the suburban neighborhoods of Gbessia, Bonfinn, Dixinn, Mafanco, La Sig, Coléyah, and Landréya. The visitors could not miss the beauty of the spectacle. As Lacouture noted so well, Conakry "offered a tremendous Negro spectacle. Songs, dances, collective rituals of women of the most picturesque sort, healers and griots imbued this Guinean welcome with a tone quite different from that of Tananarive, of Brazzaville, or Abidjan."[4] Naturally, the homages were intended as much for de Gaulle as for Sékou Touré, both living symbols of liberation and hope. The General, pleased, shared in the delight. Spontaneously, as was reported by Georges Chaffard, he turned to his host and said, "I hope it will be this nice in Dakar."

"I hope so, my General," answered the Guinean. "I hope also to behold

---

4. J. Lacouture, *Le Monde* No. 4227, August 27 1958.

with my own eyes the welcome in Senegal. For I, myself, must travel to Dakar tomorrow."

"Then, dear president," said de Gaulle, "Give me the pleasure of joining me tomorrow in my personal plane."[5]

This dialogue is evidence that the spectacle of music and dance can immerse human beings and bring them together. To all appearances, the visit in Conakry had started well. The PDG was far more skilled in culturing such a tradition of popular welcome, and they excelled in the gesture. Sékou Touré and his partisans had, for many years, made use of folkloric (and modern) songs and dances, and even of religious festivals, as weapons to settle the supremacy of their party over the land.

For the PDG, such demonstrations expressed the national culture and the hopes of the peoples. That Fodéba Kéita—grand master and choreographer of the *Ballets africains* in Paris— returned to the service of the PDG in the position of Territorial Councilor for Siguiri, from the region of Upper Guinea, and as Minister of the Interior, further strengthened the artistic orientation of the party. Art and politics became inseparable and symbiotic. For the leaders of the Guinean branch of the RDA, the notion of art for art's sake was foreign and unjustified. Fodéba conceived art as an entity that was pleasing and agreeable, but also had a goal, be it political, social, or even religious. They all felt that music carried an evocative power within itself, that invited reflection and action.

Thus, in steps through its history, the PDG shaped for itself, in all the languages of the nation, a rich and variegated repertory. Thus, it is easy to understand the organization and the spectacular order of the crowd, arrayed as in battalions on both sides, commanded by their activists, and intoning rhythmically the assigned slogans: "Independence!" and "Long life de Gaulle! Long live Sily!" while waving their banners. The welcome on that Monday, August 25, displayed, on a broad scale, the principle of complementarity between art and politics. It was also the product of the creative genius of Fodéba Kéita and the hold exercised by the PDG over the masses. There in Conakry, Fodéba benefited from the outstanding assistance of the activists—both men and women—who were experienced in the art of arousing the people. Among these activists, Bengali Camara and Mamadi Kaba, both musically gifted and both long engaged

---

5. Georges Chaffard, *op. cit.*, 194.

in the labor movement of the party, proved their abilities with their appeal to workers and in labor protests.

For that day, the activists had ensured the massive participation of the chapters of the Workers' Union for the reception of General de Gaulle. The same held true for Aïssatou Maffory Bangoura, who was already proving herself to be the *grande dame* of the Party in Conakry, and whose name was the symbol of the engagement of women. She had become known since 1952 for her gift for organization and her boldness; Monday morning, very early, she made sure that her teams of women—true brigades of Amazons, capable of spreading terror—were equipped in instructions ranging from the order to the music at strategic points along the course of the official motorcade. The combination of these elements endowed the reception offered in Conakry with a rich and flamboyant allure, grandiose and unforgettable.

Let us return to the cortege. It crossed the Tumbo Bridge that links the island of the city of Conakry to the suburbs on the mainland. At the end of the bridge, to the left, the festival was in full force, under the watchful gaze of giant hundred-year old cottonwood trees, as though the powerful chapters of the PDG from the neighborhood of Korontin nearby had come, despite their orthodox Muslim leader, the Imam El-Hadji Mohammed Lamine Kaba, to address their prayers to the divinity, Gbassi-Kolon, who, for ages, had carefully guarded the site of Conakry. The cortege followed its course to the acclamations of the crowds in Koléwondi, not far from the Cinema Vox, where Sékou Touré regularly held his meetings. The convoy continued, to the frenetic applause of the masses of inhabitants of the Manquepas and Almamiya neighborhoods, where dwelled Senegalese, Lebano-Syrians and French, at the crossroads by the Monoprix store down to the Palace Cinema and then to Avenue-Bar. Then, through the rhythmic ovations of the representatives of the quarters of Boulbinet and Sandervaliya, gathered on the space before the Cathedral and the esplanade of the Urbaine and the Seine, an apartment building with an impressive modern structure. Finally, the long train of cars stopped in the Palace of the Governor alongside the sea.

To all appearances, the visit was starting under favorable auspices. Against all expectations, the welcome in Conakry was of the warmest and most magnificent. By means of this high-quality spectacle, Sékou Touré, his party, and the other political groupings as well wished to display the maturity and the solidarity of the people of Guinea. On that day, their unity seemed real and strong. The street festival, a magical spectacle of a rare order and worthy of the great Parisian cabarets, succeeded beyond all hopes. The visitors were delighted. However, Governor Mauberna, who knew the situation in Guinea very well, had worries. In the meantime, he made sure that all the little details had been seen to.

Everything seemed to be going well at the Governor's Palace, with a refreshing breeze blowing from the ocean behind. The residence was in effervescence; the apartments were prepared. The General and his personal staff had settled in. To add an African accent, and as a sign of his esteem, Sékou Touré was lodging Cornut-Gentille, the Minister for Overseas France, and Pierre Messmer, the Governor-General of the A.O.F., in his personal residence, which should lead to a fruitful dialogue (what irony! Just three years before, it had been "war" between the PDG and the colonial administration). Cordiality was at its height, and no one questioned it.

A pragmatic and methodical mind, de Gaulle, as soon as he arrived, consulted the Governor about the situation in Conakry and about reactions to the constitutional proposal. Mauberna had a copy of the speech that Sékou Touré was to deliver. In the Governor's opinion, it would all depend on the PDG and on Sékou Touré, whose control of the country was almost total. On that topic, he added, the speech to be delivered would not cast enough light on the orientation of Guinea, for the Extraordinary Convention of the Party would determine the vote in September. "It will be 95% if the Party and Touré decide to vote 'yes' and it will also be 95% if they give the signal to vote 'no,'" he announced, offering a copy of Sékou Touré's oration with the harshest passages marked with red checks.

Amid these dealings, as planned through protocol, the arrival of Sékou Touré was announced. He came on a courtesy visit. The head of the French government and the Vice-Mayor of Conakry had not seen each other since Sékou Touré had presented the position of the RDA on August 5TH in Matignon, the residence of the prime minister in Paris. The context was no longer quite the same: there, on that day, they suffered from the oppressive heat of Conakry. The two leaders talked. Their conversation was short. Short as it was, might it have been enough to inspire confidence between two men who barely knew each other? As we know, success in politics requires a dialogue between the parties, and a mutual understanding of their ideas. What did de Gaulle and Touré say to each other? No one knows, or ever will. It remains that at the bottom of the stairway, upon his return from the General's office, Touré met Cornut-Gentille and Messmer. They were wondering what the "big boss" thought of the speech. Everything went well, it seemed, thought Touré. But, they wondered, had de Gaulle read the text?

That was the question that many observers, Guinean and foreign, were asking. For the former knew that Touré was impulsive, with a ready tongue and easily carried away by enthusiasm. The latter had some idea of the hot-tempered character of the General. Should there be the slightest misunderstanding then, it would spark a conflagration leading to an unfortunate confrontation, and, one might then claim that the deities worked together against any Franco-Guinean accord. And this would match up with a popular belief, in which the land of Guinea, because it was fabulously rich but difficult to exploit, required special prayers and blessings to mitigate and control the environment, and to appease its deities. If one credits the Guinean witnesses and the French journalists, an evil concurrence of circumstances left its mark upon the General's visit to Guinean soil that day.

First, Conakry had not originally been planned on the General's itinerary. Once again, it was Bernard Cornut-Gentille, a tireless supporter of Sékou Touré, who thought of making a stop in Conakry "to flatter his man in Conakry," and to create a "warmer atmosphere, favorable to secret discussions." The point was to appease the PDG and to destroy any secessionist tendency; the intention was most laudable, given Touré's influence in West Africa.

Houphouët, unwavering in his judgment of Sékou Touré's temperament, looked askance upon this stop in Guinea, and had doubts about Cornut-Gentille's motives. Paul-Henri Siriex reported Houphouët's statement that "in my absence, M. Cornut-Gentille—whose petty and resentful mind I had begun to grasp—is doing his best to "throw banana-peels before my feet." He went to see the General, to explain that he only represented the right wing of the RDA. And thus, in a final effort to "retrieve" Sékou Touré—was it proper to stop in Conakry?—the General, for his part, had no reason to think that Sékou Touré pursued other goals and was playing a game of double-cross. And so, he accepted the stop in Conakry."[6] (What would that double-cross have been? Neither Houphouët nor his biographer give an explanation. Did Houphouët suppose that Touré was following a line different from that of the majority of the RDA after he met de Gaulle on August 5, in the name of the Party?)

And then, the text of Sékou Touré's speech posed problems. Governor Mauberna had read it and found it hard and even clumsy in certain passages. Therefore, early in the morning, he and Touré took advantage of a forced stop of the plane that was bringing Gabriel d'Arboussier from Abidjan to Dakar, to sift and pare down the text. (Touré respected and admired d'Arboussier.) But even so, on his return, the Guinean leader proved unable to consider the suggestions and the corrections due to a lack of time. As a third point, the de Gaulle-Sily encounter had not be properly prepared on either side. The two men had met for the first time barely three weeks before. They did not know each other; each was a stranger to the other. Sékou Touré was used to the politicians of the Fourth Republic, but knew nothing of the personality of de Gaulle, a veteran accustomed to military command and deference. De Gaulle reflected an air of grandeur and was naturally imposing; he had all the traits of a chief, of a certain period, accustomed to give orders, or to listen to the calm and reflective recommendations delivered in a formal context by obsequious interlocutors. The General abhorred unpredictability in political positions, as well as ideological speeches. He had no idea of the unfettered temperament of the charismatic young Guinean leader, nor of his labor-inspired rhetoric.

Cornut-Gentille and Pierre Messmer were much more familiar with Touré; they had seen his text, and while they disapproved of its tone, they had not had the opportunity to prepare de Gaulle. Jacques Foccart was de Gaulle's closest advisor on this subject, but he had been out of sight since his arrival in Conakry: a serious security issue kept him busy in a discreet wing of the Governor's Palace. Misunderstandings loomed large ahead, and it was difficult to avoid them and to ensure the success of the stop in Conakry. Confrontation seemed inevitable, despite the resounding splendor of the greeting. De Gaulle and Touré both seemed well-intentioned, but they had very different styles. As the meeting would take place, the

---

6. Quoted in Paul-Henri Siriex, *Houphouët-Boigny ou la sagesse africaine* (Paris: Nathan and NEA, 1986), 180.

Territorial Assembly would be transformed into a gladiatorial arena in which two men, very different in age and experience, but who, in truth, did not seek conflict, would, like Roman gladiators, engage in an unforeseen struggle. Such a shock would have heavy consequences, especially for Guinea; the territory still lacked adequate means for its development.

The two fighters—both gifted in their abilities and impassioned for their respective causes—would each give proof of their skills, or preferably, their undeniable superiority, in a cut-and-thrust duel of brilliant and memorable oratory. The joust that they would have hoped to avoid would transform General de Gaulle's stop in Conakry, along with the speech delivered by Sékou Touré, into one of the signature moments in the history of French decolonization in Africa.

As the Assembly stood very close to the Governor's Palace, the official cortege, with some pleasure, decided to make its way on foot. The visitors admired the shaded avenues and the elegant sidewalks of the Administrative quarter, marked by a light sea breeze. As had occurred on the Route du Niger, a large crowd of Europeans and Africans was showing its joy through cries of "Vive de Gaulle! Vive Sily!" Friendly voices speaking African languages raised themselves, addressing Sékou Touré; he answered them with a glittering smile. There could have been no better illustration of the pluralism and the symbiosis of colonial society than the spectacle of this cortege made up of white men, of various origins, of metis, and of Black Africans dressed in fine formal clothing in European or African styles.

The contrast between the General's uniform and Sékou Touré's *boubou* reflected the difference between the cultures of Europe and the Africa of tropical savannas, an opposition that colonization and the colonial schools made great efforts to smooth out and harmonize. Each of the two men, in his own way, was impressive and radiant. De Gaulle wore a light khaki suit; he was tall and erect and rode over the crowd with a hieratic effect. He was undeniably the incarnation of Free France (in the war time) and no less certainly the hope for a renewal of the French nation, showing on the horizon. And in the assured and composed stride of Sékou Touré, one also saw something special but intangible. On that afternoon, in a flowing *boubou*, gleaming white and delicately kept in place by his left hand, he shone out with a brilliant aureole that reflected the elegance that belongs to youth, the force of a magnet, the grace of his communion with the people of Guinea and Conakry, and the profile of the predestined man who immediately crossed through the portal of historical maturity. Quite unexpectedly, a *jeli* (griot) from Upper Guinea crossed the street, called to him, and then sang melodiously:

This day is a great day!

Make this day your own!

It is the first of the three sublime days inscribed in the register of the fate of every man.

Sékou Touré was young, flamboyant, and talented; the eyes and the hope of a yet-unborn nation were turned to him—a heavy load, perhaps too heavy for one man alone, and who so far had not yet faced great trials. Slowly, the cortege came to the Assembly—a modest building in colonial style, but extremely meaningful. Many hours before, the building had been occupied by a throng of dignitaries and of ordinary citizens. Muggy heat filled the room. The dignitaries settled in their seats, and the session opened.

Saïfoulaye Diallo, a *député* and the Chair of the Territorial Assembly, was notable for his very slender and slightly bowed size, his fine-featured face, and the copper tone of his skin. He rose to speak. In sober and serene tones, he welcomed the people of Conakry, General de Gaulle, and the General's suite. Without great formality, he set the tone and raised the "subject, which was to offer necessary clarifications." He "rejoiced that deferrals and confusion would finally make way for bold decisions, without qualifiers."

The speaker chose his language deliberately and pronounced words fraught with meaning. What did he insinuate with the terms "deferrals" and "clarifications" at a moment one week after so many speeches given in Africa by the General on those questions? To make his thoughts clearer, calmly, he stressed the importance that current events held for Franco-African relations. Thus, he wished for de Gaulle to make some bold and specific statement, in agreement with his own tradition and the needs of the moment, meaning the needs of African Nationalism, whose emergence he, Saïfoulaye, greeted proudly. Further, he described the Guinean leaders as "patriots resolved to work for the well-being of their African homeland" and to "assume their responsibility towards history, for they were strengthened by the unconditional support of the peoples, who also were well-aware of the importance of the options to be taken." Governor Mauberna had suggested this earlier.

In corroboration of this point, Saïfoulaye drew a historical parallel between displays of patriotism, in one case that of the French against the Nazis during the Second World War, and in the present time, that of colonized Africans. Following this sketch, de Gaulle, who established and directed the Resistance in France, "will understand, better than any other French leader, the legitimacy of African Nationalism, because of his experience in resistance, and certainly, because of the high qualities that he embodies." Saïfoulaye honored patriotism as a principle of political solidarity, "the reliable warrant of an enduring attachment that was grounded in a free and fraternal association, on equal footing," between France and Africa. In conclusion, he announced that Sékou Touré, Chair of the Council of Government, would lay out in its broad lines the perspective of Guinea on current affairs and issues.

Commentators have neglected this short speech, but Saïfoulaye Diallo's words had indisputable worth. First, the man was reflective, moved by a spirit of duty and love of his land; he was, in truth, a great leader. His authority and his prestige, far from casting into shade the qualities of Sékou Touré, his companion in the struggle, were complementary, in a form of symbiosis. Diallo possessed the arts of reassurance and concision. His speech was clear and straight-forward and followed the lines of history without giving offence. His propositions, a preface to the speech that Sékou Touré would give, were content to suggest without stating. In that year, 1958, such was the character of the somewhat two-headed leadership of Guinea. Complementary in action and in temperament, Sékou Touré and Saïfoulaye Diallo—to whom one might well add the names of Lansana Béavogui, Moussa Diakité, and Lansana Diané—were exemplars at that time of the essential qualities of the PDG. As one harrows a field before sowing the seed, the text of Saïfoulaye Diallo prepared the audience for the expression of the thoughts of the leader of the PDG, and—yes, we must say so—for the storm that loomed.

Now, it was Sily's turn to speak. With controlled movement, he rose and made his way to the podium, applauded by all.

And he started. Like a torrent swollen with floodwaters, he poured forth his waves with vigor and vehemence; they spread in all directions. His voice rose, whirled through philosophy and history, the fields of human dignity and of Pan-Africanism. Then the voice landed on the soil of Guinea, bounced into the gardens of a Franco-African union; then it launched anew into the sphere of mutual recognition of political rights, and finally, it settled on the prospect of great unions. The horizon was vast and tumultuous. The didactic tone only barely addressed the immediate agenda and the occasion of the General's visit.

The speech had much of a metaphysical treatise and a list of grievances, the whole charged with electricity. In the first part of his allocution, following the enlightened philosophers of the 18TH century, the speaker took pleasure in lofty words about general ideas such as fate, history, well-being, liberty, progress, and the hero as though to communicate a philosophical and political message. The allocution and the learning impressed the public that came numerous from Conakry and beyond. The tone, the voice—rocket-like—propelled the orator into a sphere aureoled with the deeds and thoughts of the revolutionaries that slaked the thirst of some activists and young Africans. The myth of Sékou Touré—meaning the transformation of his image into that of the bard and symbol of African dignity, and even of a great leader of the Third World— was born at that precise moment. Truly, for some, that speech might be compared to a battlefield on which he earned his place in history. Yet, the discourse is multifaceted.

From the very start of his speech, Touré set forth the value of man in general, and that of the man of action and the hero in particular. This specific idea proved judicious, there in the Territorial Assembly, for all eyes turned to the illustrious leader of the French Resistance. Like musical notes in a harmonious progression came the lyrical appeal of the speaker toward the visitor: "*Monsieur le Président*, you have come to Africa preceded by a double privilege: you are part of a glorious legend that magnifies the victory of liberty over subjection, and you are the first leader of the government of the Republic to treat the soil of Guinea. Your presence among us is a symbol not only of the 'Resistance' that brought about the triumph of reason over force, the victory of good over evil. Your presence also—I may even say principally—represents a new stage, a new decisive period, a new phase in evolution." It seems difficult not to respond to such well-chosen words, and to see them as appropriate, eloquent, and touching.

However, discordant notes soon emerged. Without any segue, the speaker launched the theme of the need to reclaim the values of the "African people, living day-to-day in the hope of seeing their dignity respected." The speaker allowed that this allusion could not apply to de Gaulle, who in France's most difficult hours had remained the arbiter and witness to the value of Africans. Why then say such things? The speech became a plea in favor of the emancipation of Africa and Guinea, a plea that was perhaps, at that moment, unnecessary. Through that plea, though, Touré most likely wished to present himself as the spokesman for African unity.

Following that point, with no connecting thoughts, Touré turned to the "needs of evolution and human emancipation" to explain why Africa lagged behind—because of "economic and political structures inherited from a colonial regime that is out of balance with the current situation and the aspirations for the future." In his words, colonization brought forth poverty, and moral disorder. Touré put forth these ideas on historic and sociological order as celestial truths. The boldness of these statements electrified the crowd filling the galleries, the stairs, and the street, and brought forth immediate applause. The communion with the crowd led the speaker, unconsciously, to turn his back on his guest from time to time to face the public, as though he were making a union speech, a labor-oriented propaganda. The closer his body and soul came to the audience, the greater the divide between himself and the General became. The accusing and didactic tone and the length of the speech were hard for the General to bear. Exasperated, he did not hide his impatience. He felt tired, and even injured. However, he had to endure the second part of the speech. And this part, Touré presented the demands of the people.

The second section displayed all the characteristic formulas and the usual rhetoric commonly used by Sékou Touré. He presented himself as the intrepid hero of African nationalism, the defender of the great aggregations, without which Africa would face a perilous future. Of course, he also wished to present himself as a sincere friend to France. How could he reconcile these two points? It was a most challenging task. Thereafter, he tackled the question of under-development, and offered an apologia for poverty and for dignity, in a style that showed singular skill in the rhetorical style of labor-oriented speakers. This style allowed him to manipulate both common sense and the commonalities of political sociology.

The orator could not stop there. He was swept up in the ardent passion of his speech and of his effect on the crowds in the hall, the corridors, and the adjoining chambers. And so, he cried out an unforgettable phrase, a succinct formula that struck like a spark cast from an incandescent torch: "*We prefer poverty in freedom to wealth in enslavement!*" It fell among the acclamations of a mesmerized crowd.

For many people, that statement—really a formula and a bomb—constituted the essence of the speech of August 25 in Conakry, although several other terms also defined it. The strong and proud statement laid down a challenge, and, therefore, it has been quoted ever since. It launched the legend of Sékou Touré. It also brought heavy consequences. The more so because neediness—while possessing a virtuous and respectable aspect—always severely tests the abilities of the peoples in poverty; and poverty continues to expose the weakness of a state lacking resources. Might not the future generations of a Guinea suffering from under-development lament this presumption? However, the statement will forever confirm the view of Sékou Touré that will be preserved by history, i.e., the image of a brave and principled man, one with great dreams.

In the next section, Touré presented arguments in favor of decolonization. Breaching protocol, he even quoted the speech he had given some months before, before Gérard Jaquet, the former Minister for Overseas France. From that point on, the tone moved into a crescendo and became polemical, with biting observations and displays of his fist on the lectern. Like a *sofa* ("brave warrior," in Maninka), he attacked the colonial spirit, the trickery, and the depersonalization. The listeners, awe-struck, answered with an avalanche of applause when he burst out and hammered out the words of another statement: "*We shall not give up—we shall never give up—our legitimate and natural right to independence!*" Touré was then at the height of the eloquence that was always a base of his popularity. The terms he had used were bitter and cutting, and perhaps inappropriate, especially after the speeches de Gaulle had made in Brazzaville and in Abidjan. Was he not offending the sensibilities of his famous French guest? However, he was unable to restrain his tongue. He repeated that he attached little importance to the name that might be applied to a Franco-African association, and thus, almost locked out further dialogue.

Controlling himself, as in a musical work where the Pastorale follows the storm, Tourè tempered his tone and offered elegant and captivating remarks about the union between France and Africa. "Our hearts and our reason, besides our most obvious interests, will lead us to choose, without any hesitation, independence and freedom in this union, rather than defining ourselves without France or even against France." It is an open question whether General de Gaulle took it as intended. The voice of Sékou Touré and the outbursts of applause it aroused were further elements likely to antagonize his interlocutor, who from that point, displayed indifference and distance. Sékou Touré's eloquence was an invitation to a breach.

Let us consider Sily's speech further. His thoughts encompassed the great framework of the nationalist movement blowing across Africa. Here and there, the clusters of his ideas became entangled, as though in a labyrinth. Trying to say everything, he caused at least some offense. His speech can be compared to a dense, thicketed forest, mixing splendid essences with more ordinary species. Such a combination was a sign of weakness. It may have reflected the involvement of many of the officials of the PDG in the drafting of the text, as was reported by a journalist writing for *Le Monde*.

Such a statement draws our attention. During a broadcast of *Mémoires d'un continent* (Memories of a Continent), which was a once-popular program on RFI (Radio France Inter) hosted by Ibrahima Kaké, Saliou Camara, then with the Guinean radio, and four former leaders of the PDG stated that a commission of six members had composed the speech. The leaders were El-Hadji Mamadou Fofana, Deen Oumar Camara, Mory Camara, and Fodé-Lamine Touré. Béla Doumbouya of Mamou, another veteran of the PDG, in turn, confirmed this opinion, and added that the original version of the speech, from the pen of Sékou Touré himself, was even more virulent.[7] For his part, Cheikh Chérif, former director of Radio-Conakry and a former ambassador to the USSR, who at one time had been very close to the leader of the PDG, recalled the influence of Sékou Kaba, a lawyer also known as Kabakarou Sékou, on Sékou Touré. Kaba pursued excellent studies in law in Paris and passed—brilliantly—the bar examination for Paris. Like Fodéba Kéita, he lived in the

---

7. Kaké, *op. cit.*, 79.

3RD Arrondissement of Paris. A devotee of Marxism, Kaba, as we may recall, was well-known in the world of the Africans of the Quartier Latin (Left Bank of Paris). On his return to Guinea in 1957, he opened a law office and mixed with the circle of political leaders. According to Chérif, Master Kaba made suggestions and revisions to the text. Some passages of the speech look back directly to the classics of Communism.

On the other hand, N'Faly Sangaré—a Paris School of law graduate and former Governor of the Central Bank, and close to the Guinean leader—maintained that Touré would not accept the writings of others, and especially not those of a commission. In Sangaré's opinion, the speech of August 25TH was an authentic reflection of "Sékou Touré, the labor leader, the politician, and the author of the speech delivered to the Fourth Convention of the PDG." This argument is not irrelevant. To settle the question, however, we may simply note that Touré did, sometimes, consult other persons.

The hall offered loud applause to Touré when he ended his speech. The hall welcomed General de Gaulle with an equal fervor when he rose to speak. With heavy step, perhaps somewhat tired, his gaze distant, he moved to the podium. The audience was fascinated by the man's profile and was hypnotized at the sight of a living hero. They roused themselves, and once again, applauded loudly. The slow delivery and the determination—both intentional—of the low and serious voice left no one undeceived for long. A great historic moment was about to take place.

First, observing the proprieties, the visitor expressed his gratitude to the people of Conakry for the "magnificent welcome" that, he said, symbolized "a great attachment to France." This point was important to him, as a major figure of that country. He also was delighted that the people, quite fairly, offered "no reproaches" to France. With this preliminary observation, an indirect response to Sékou Touré, he sketched out a picture of what French colonization had contributed to the development of Guinea. This was his way of rejecting the diatribes. Then, in the peremptory tone that was a characteristic trait and that could make use of history, he stated, "There is indeed no reason for France to blush for anything, in the work that she has accomplished here with Africans." There was applause in the room.

With pride, and perhaps some condescendence, de Gaulle continued this argument; he alluded to the beauty of the city of Conakry, to the quality of the expression—*en français*—of the two speeches delivered by Diallo and Touré, and to the richness of the ideas presented by the two Guinean leaders. The remark subtly reinforced his theme of the work "accomplished with Africans." De Gaulle saw in Sékou Touré, despite his glistening *boubou* and his skull cap, a product of French civilization, as this latter had demonstrated through his eloquence, his breadth of knowledge, and his "truly French passion," as he stressed. The General felt that these qualities should invite homage to French colonial action as well as to the contribution of the Africans themselves. The reminder of this collaboration, that had been mutually fruitful in the past, led him to suggest the possibility of a new form of cooperation in the future, within the bosom of the community, as his voyage was meant to suggest.

Then, with imperturbable emphasis and aplomb, de Gaulle offered corrections. His answers came easily and with irony. Without qualifiers, in the name of France, he guaranteed to Africans their "free determination," but he also urged the Guinean leaders toward greater realism, for, he said, "We live upon an earth and in a world in which realities rule, as they have always done." This realism, he added, applied as much to the "Africa that is new" as to the "France that is also always new" (and here, the speaker was making direct reference to his return to power and to the general spirit of renovation that was moving France).

Then, the General tackled the "fundamental question that is quite simply to know whether between us, Africans and Metropolitans, we wish to engage together in a Community." Skilled in the art of the riposte, the orator assured that the initiative for such a union belonged to France, and to her alone. With further vigor, he emphatically added that "No one is forced to join."

Riding the movement, this man-at-arms, the imperial ruler of the new France retorted, with furor that is not easily forgotten, "Independence has been mentioned. I shall say here more loudly than elsewhere that Independence is within reach of Guinea. Guinea can achieve it on September 28, by voting "No" to the proposal presented to her. In that case, I promise that the Metropolis shall offer no obstacle. There may indeed be consequences, but there shall be no obstacles, and your Territory may, as you wish and under the conditions you choose, follow the path you may choose."

Fervent applause and shivers of excitement rang throughout the hall.

Did the crowd truly understand? It was, however, transported more by the eloquence than by the content of the message. How could one not respond to this verbal force—this oratorical art, perhaps—that most artistically linked, in simple and clear terms, following the rules and subtleties of the language, both pride and threats? De Gaulle wielded warnings. He blew hot and cold with all the skill of a master of speech (and of the pen). He left it, without any doubts, up to the Guineans to vote according to their conscience. The significance and the tone of the speech define it as a rare document in the annals of French decolonization.

Did de Gaulle, deep down, wish for a rupture with Guinea? Wasn't his reply guided by spite and arrogance? Did he intend to show that France could do very well without Guinea? One might say that he could understand the excesses in language and the youth of Sékou Touré, and that de Gaulle was offering him his hand. For, unlike Cartier, for example, who felt that Africa largely represented a burden, de Gaulle basically felt that Africa represented a choice asset in France's foreign relations. There was nothing surprising about this. This, no doubt, could explain the spirit of dialogue and collaboration.

There in the sweltering humidity of Conakry, de Gaulle had exchanged his military uniform for the more humane garb of the tutor and the man of experience. Even better, he was sharing his wisdom with youth, driven by fervency. He put aside the martial and impressive tones of the Man of the Sword, to use the soft and reassuring voice of the schoolmaster, as can well be seen in the following passage, in which the General pointed to solidarity to overcome poverty and prejudice:

This community—if we create it together—will be an act of faith in a destiny that will be common to us and humane, and it will also be, I truly believe, the means, the only means to establish practical collaboration for the many people who are our responsibility. I believe that Guinea will say 'yes' to France, and I believe that a road will open before us, on which we may walk together. The road will not be easy; there will be many obstacles on the path faced by the men of today, and words can do nothing to change that. We must, however, overcome those obstacles. We must make our way past the obstacle of poverty. Other obstacles

will arise from our passions, our prejudices, our exaggerations. I
believe that we can overcome those obstacles as well.

In his own fashion, de Gaulle was trying to push, to convince Touré of
the necessity of accepting the Referendum, especially for the future of
Guinea. Did Touré grasp the appeal that seemed almost a supplication?
Speaking in this tone, de Gaulle calmed the growing tensions within
the hall. The spontaneous character of the speech helped reinforce the
impression of sincerity, and to present an image of the General that differed from the hermetic and hieratic mien that was usually attributed to
him. The spontaneity, the more human tones of the answer may perhaps
explain why the text of this speech was not included in the collection of
de Gaulle's speeches, published in 1970, for the passage displays a noble,
even poignant feeling. There, de Gaulle delivered a brief ode in honor of
Franco-Guinean solidarity.

To erase any confusion, and to establish harmony, de Gaulle, once
again, stressed the importance of the union in language that was always
clear and in tones that did not hide his feelings. Such an openness on his
part was somewhat surprising when he added, "It is in that spirit that I
have come to talk to you in this Assembly, and I spoke with confidence,
because I firmly believe in a future that assemblies of men can form, and
that those men will be able to bring forth from the earth and from human
nature what is needed to make men better and happier in the world. For
should it happen that we were divided, all the imperialism in the world
would trample us."

In this passage, de Gaulle wished to show himself as prophetic and as a
realist. Therefore, he stressed the utility of cooperation for development,
and resisted, a second time, the temptation to ennoble poverty and want.
He was a realist. A man of thought and a man of action, he ended this
part of his speech with a phrase, worthy in its concision of the soldier: "I
have spoken. You will reflect."

Finally, concluding his speech, de Gaulle invited the elite of Guinea
to speak in favor of the YES, and almost in a pitiful manner, once again,
extended his hand with the supreme hope of returning in a few months.
This last phrase was a solicitation, almost the last. Alas! Moved by the
realism that comes to men of full experience, de Gaulle then collected
himself and added, "And should I not come back to see you, please know

that the memory of my visit to this lovely, noble, and great city of the future—that is a memory that I shall not lose."

The weather on that day was wonderful, shining and glorious. By chance, it was in Conakry that the General de Gaulle delivered the greatest speech of his African tour, a speech that is perhaps one of the most moving in the Gaullean repertory. With an iron fist in a velvet glove, on the spot, but with great skill, he managed to wield the martial tone and patriotism, rhetorical skill with an openness to dialogue, wisdom, and understanding. His spontaneous speech and the prepared speech of Sékou Touré were each proof of different temperaments, of course, but also showed common points in patriotism and solidarity. De Gaulle extended his hand; Sékou Touré hesitated.

Following his speech, amid the warm ovations of the audience, General de Gaulle returned to his seat at his pace of a weary giant, his gaze so distant that he forgot his *képi* on the podium (it was retrieved by Émile Tompapa, a well-known leader of the boy-scouts in the Catholic mission and on Guinean radio). The session was adjourned, and without any disturbance, the audience rose and allowed the dignitaries to retire. Sékou Touré took a seat next to de Gaulle in the official car. What might they have said to each other on the drive back to the Governor's Palace? No one knows. The General was irritated.

No sooner had Sékou Touré left to Governor's Palace than de Gaulle summoned a small council with Cornut-Gentille, Messmer, and Governor Mauberna. In an arid tone that clearly showed dissatisfaction, he commented, "Well, gentlemen, there is a man with whom we can never reach agreement. Therefore, there is nothing more to be done here. Come, it's quite clear. We will depart on the morning of September 29" (the day after the Referendum). As the three advisers tried to assuage him, he retorted in even more cutting tones, "What! Won't the administrators and the military obey?"

"Yes, of course, *mon Général,*" answered the Governor. "But what about the French interests in Guinea?"

"Are you telling me that Guinea is indispensable to France? No. There are places that are indispensable to us, countries that must remain united with us: Algeria, for example. But Guinea? Let her choose, let her take the consequences."

Thereafter, the atmosphere was tense and marked by bad temper. Like a great beast, wounded and at bay, the General avoided any uncomfortable contacts. He withdrew his promise to take Sékou Touré to Dakar in his own plane the next day. He ate alone and refused any interviews during the reception planned for that evening in the Governor's quarters. Highlighting the break that had begun, Cornut-Gentille, Minister for Overseas France, and Messmer, Governor-General of the AOF, moved out of Sékou Touré's residence.

That evening, during the reception, the atmosphere was icy. The Guinean leader, now dressed in a fine European-style outfit, exchanged some remarks here and there. Jean Lacoutoure, the correspondent for *Le Monde*, snagged him in passing and asked questions: "Is it an aggressive YES or a NO?"

"What we want is a true marriage. A marriage among equals must include the possibility of divorce. We want that right on our part to be recognized formally. The right to separate, however, does not imply the desire to separate."

"But the General acknowledged that right in Brazzaville," said the reporter.

"Is the right specified in the constitution? To the contrary—the text mentions only the penalties for secession. We want liberty; we are promised punishment."

"You would take the risk of conflict with your friends in the RDA, the risk of destroying the unity of the Party?"

"What does the RDA matter, when all of Africa is at stake?"[8]

Sily had lost nothing of his combative tone nor his identification with the larger African cause, as he perceived it. His self-confidence was impermeable. He remained alert and brilliant; he could offer an African explanation to this Franco-Guinean collision. On August 25, through his organization of the masses, the audacity of his language and the force of his speech, he gained a privileged place within the circle of Third-World nationalists.

During the reception, despite some hesitations on either part, de Gaulle and Touré finally came together. As by magic, the space around them emptied. What did they say to each other? Sékou Touré's account

---

8. Jean Lacouture, *Cinq hommes et la France* (Paris: Seuil, 1961), 352-53.

is unknown to us: none knows it or ever shall. The General, for his part, offered an account in the following terms in his *Mémoires d'espoir*:

Make no mistake!" I told him. "You are no longer dealing with the French Republic of the past.... For the France of today, colonialism is done with. This means that she is indifferent to your reproaches about the past. Henceforth, she is willing to offer her support to the state that you shall become. But France expects to make ends meet. France has long lived without Guinea. France shall continue to live on, even were they to be separated. And on that supposition, it is a given that we would immediately withdraw our assistance.... I would add that given the bonds that have united our two countries, you should have no doubt that a 'No!', formally voted against the solidarity that France offers you, would mean that our relations would be stripped of the conditions of friendship and preference among other world states.[9]

This text, composed long after the moment, tells nothing of Touré's reaction in this last *tête-à-tête*.

De Gaulle could not have been more precise. Still, we should stress that on the topic of the colonial accounts, de Gaulle expressed ideas that came close to Cartiériste views, but without the chauvinistic undertones or the desire for a complete break between the partners. He felt that the colonies were no longer a profitable enterprise, and that the time had come to be done with the myth of exploitative, destructive, and racist colonialism. The visitor felt that the idea of abandoning a colony was neither impossible nor wrong. In his opinion, decolonization counted in the order of things to think about.

For the visiting speaker in Conakry, decolonization could lead—under a far different form from that of traditional colonialist piracy—to a cooperation in political perspectives and in development, to a dialogue of civilizations, and all that might well serve the interests of France on the international scale. This can explain, in part, why de Gaulle dwelled on cooperation and solidarity. However, Touré, proclaiming a populist Marxism, did not see matters in that way.

---

9. De Gaulle, *op. cit.*, 60-61.

Let us go back to August 25. Later in the evening, Cornut-Gentille, who had brought about this stop in Conakry, tried to mend the broken crockery. His efforts went for nothing. Sékou Touré was not to be moved. The visit to Conakry proved, in the end, a failure. All told, the magnificence of the welcome stretching from the airport to the city proved no indication of the drama that unfolded in the Assembly and in the Governor's Palace. The consequence of a tragic misunderstanding, a failure in comprehension between two proud and obstinate characters, the opposition of two energetic symbols.

The next morning, under a rainy sky, through empty streets, General de Gaulle and his suite made their way back to the Gbessia-Conakry Airport. In the official car, neither the General nor his Guinean host unclenched their teeth. Following the honors paid by a military detachment under the wing of the plane, the man of the Cross of Lorraine extended his hand to Sily and said, "Farewell to Guinea!" Governor Mauberna was summoned into the plane; he was instructed to inform Guinean authorities that France would choose to separate from Guinean on September 29. The decision had been taken, clearly and definitely. The break had been accomplished. The Caravelle blazoned with the Cross of Lorraine lifted off and headed for Cape Verde. Did Sily have any emotions of worry or regret? To all appearances, no. He had spoken his thoughts aloud. At any rate, the die was cast, and preparations were underway for the final clash on September 28.

CHAPTER 4
GUINEA ON THE EVE OF THE REFERENDUM

L IKE A HURRICANE, General de Gaulle's marathon travels across French-speaking Africa shook the foundations of political life through all the territories. In Conakry, the probability of a massive vote against the constitutional proposal, and consequently, a rupture with France, seemed certain. Along, perhaps, with Niger, Guinea stood out as a hard case, whose leaders were determined to make the vote on September 28 a demonstration for African unity and dignity. Such a position, however, presented something of a paradox, in that most of the other territories saw the Referendum quite differently, although they too had a firm attachment to dignity.

A retrospective view of the territory might well explain the confidence of the leaders in Conakry, along with specific aspects of Guinean politics. What was the condition of Guinea in that year of 1958? To answer that question, we need not review the entire recent political history of the land, but to outline the general aspects of the situation on the eve of the Referendum.

A fully adequate response would demand examination of the environment, the events, the resources, the social forces, and the major cultural issues. A view of the whole matters for the concept of the nation. This whole is to be understood as more than a geographical entity, or a group of people speaking the same language, and linked through the bonds of religion and social and historical forces. The territory, of course, had internationally recognized geographic limits. The borders of Guinea, as shall be shown below, were defined by a division of territories by the future colonial powers and look back to agreements that France signed with the United Kingdom, with Portugal and with Liberia during the 19TH century and at the start of the 20TH century. These borders were arbitrary, as was the case everywhere else in Africa and Asia. The agreements paid no attention to physical geography nor to the historic settlement of ethnic groups within the regions.

Because of the imposed amalgam of peoples within a new administrative entity, Guinea represented a fine example of a political creation born from colonial action and established long after the development of precolonial inter-ethnic relationships. The colony took its definite form during the 1880s, and especially after the defeat of the Almami Samori Touré in 1898, which led to a vast reconfiguration of the French lands of along upper Senegal and Niger rivers—the territory known as *Haut-Sénégal-Niger*.

At the start of the colonial era, the territorial unit that became French Guinea included societies with different political and religious traditions. In the north-west, for instance, one found stateless societies such as the Conioagui and the Bassari, along with several forest-dwelling communities in the south-east. There were also societies with an advanced state-based society, such as the Manding, whose traditions went back to ancient Wagadu and 13TH century Mali, or the Fula (Peuls), who in the 18TH century established an Islamic theocracy in the Futa-Jallon, working with the Manding Muslims; there were also the many Susu chiefdoms along the coast that were culturally and ethnically linked with the Manding peoples. Within these parameters, French Guinea—a territory about half the size of France, about 250,000 km²—developed within the framework of the AOF up to 1958.

Despite the cultural and historical differences, Guinea assumed the role of an area of contact between the Africa of the savannas (north and north-east), and the Africa of tropical forests, an area between the highly Muslim world and that of indigenous faiths—a place of meetings and understanding. The position of the colony and its natural environment contributed greatly to this characteristic. This means basically that the land of Guinea was receptive to the contact and the coexistence of movements and to the collaboration of peoples.

Seen from an airplane, geographically, the territory seems a collection of plateaus and valleys. The coastal regions are defined by sea-board plains, known as Basse Guinée or Maritime Guinea. They are separated from the interior by an escarpment: this abrupt rise in the terrain leads to the mountainous zone stretching from the east, and defines the Futa-

Jallon in the northwest, and the Forest Zones in the south-east. To the south-east, between the Futa and the forest, lies the alluvial basin of the Niger river and its affluents, an area known as Upper Guinea. Guinea defines itself as a territory with relatively high altitudes, and thus, abundant precipitation.

The four natural regions complement each other. The distribution of ethnic groups across the country does not match up exactly with the geographic divisions. In 1958, every town— Conakry, Kindia, Boké, Mamou, Labé, Youkounkoun, Dabola, Kankan, Beyla, Kissidougou, and N'Zérékoré—presented a multi-ethnic physiognomy, although one local group was predominant. Integration of the ethnic groups and their cultures was under way, thanks to the railway, to the regional roads, to the inter-regional commerce, and to the effect of monotheism, particularly that of Islam. Maritime Guinea, comparable to the Finistère in France as an outlying and isolated area, is a broad alluvial plain, watered by coastal rivers such as the Konkouré, of moderate size but with a powerful flow. It is a region of constant humidity and enormous rainfall and offers great opportunities for rice-growing and for tropical fruits. It is also a region rich in iron ore and bauxite. Maritime Guinea offers enormous industrial potential. The lowlands and the swamps are suitable for growing rice and for a plantation economy. Some plains, for example, are developed with the goal of increasing the rice-farming activity, especially along the coast, in the administrative *Cercle* of Forécariah to the south of Conakry, along the estuaries of the Soumouya and Mellacoré rivers, around the island of Kabak, and in the coastal plain of Monchon in the *Cercle* of Boffa.

The creation of the railway running from Conakry to Kankan, the proximity of the port of Conakry, and the later development of the port of Benty on the estuary of the Mellacoré, along with the establishment of other landing stages, encouraged the production of bananas, pineapples, and other tropical fruits such as oranges in the labor-intensive plantations belonging to the Europeans, the Levantines, and an emerging class of African planters. In 1958, Guinea was the principal producer of those fruits in the AOF.

Maritime Guinea was also known for its enormous deposits of bauxite and iron ore on the coast, along the Islands of Loos; in 1953, exploitation of these resources began there and, in the region, north of Boké. In 1955, plans were underway for a dam on the Konkouré, and, therefore, these deposits presented great economic possibilities. Early in the 1950s, the *Compagnie minière de Conakry* (Mining Company of Conakry) had begun to exploit the deposits on the Kaloum peninsula, considered one of the largest deposits in the world. In 1958, the authorities were planning an open-air mine on the deposits of Yomboéli, in the district of Moussaya in the *Cercle* of Forécariah. Thus, Guinea in general, and Basse-Guinée in particular, stood out in their potential for the development of electro-metallurgy and manufacturing.

Geography and history soon drew into Maritime Guinea peoples from various traditions. For centuries, the Susu people, culturally linked with the great Manding/Malinke family, have occupied the principal zones of the region, as a community of farmers, traders, Muslim preachers, and intermediaries with the Europeans. The Susu also absorbed local autochthonous groups, such as the Baga, the Landouma, and the Nalou, along with new-comer groups such as the Mikiforé (kin to the Malinké-Jallonké who had been forced out of the Futa Jallon in the 18TH century), the Moréaka, native to the Bateh, the Muslim state of Kankan-Baté in Upper Guinea, and the Ballante, who had come out of Bissau. Basse-Guinée (Lower Guinea) proves itself a true melting-pot. Economic growth and urban expansion further accentuated the pluralism and made the coastal areas the starting point for the first political movements and activism, and specifically, the rise of the PDG.

Middle Guinea, also known as the Futa Jallon, is a collection of massive rock formations and high plateaus divided by deep valleys. Many rivers—the Gambia, the Bafing (that becomes the Senegal), and the Niger, among others—spring from this region that well deserves its title of the "water tower" of West Africa. The Futa Jallon highlands offer resources for pastoralism, tourism, and for hydro-electric energy that are not to be dismissed. The terrain and the climate determine the variety of soils and landscapes, and hence, for forms of agricultural exploitation. Rice is grown in the rich and deep soils, and fonio (a type of millet) in the valleys where the soil is poorer. The grazing lands are extensive.

The favorable conditions for livestock, and especially cattle, explain the successive movements of migration that led to settlement by non-Muslim Fula herders among the sedentary Jallonké, beginning in the 14TH century, even before the spread of the Manding Empire of Mali. Later, at the start of the 18TH century, new waves of immigration brought groups of Muslim Fula herders from southern Senegal and from the Massina in the Soudan (modern Mali). The Islamic movement launched by these newcomers, with the cooperation of Maninka Muslims, transformed the human geography of the Futa. During the colonial era, all along the railway line, banana plantations spread through the valleys and up the slopes, coloring the landscape with a great verdant beauty.

The Futa Jallon and its lateritic plateau count among the sources of bauxite, of which Guinea is one of the main world producers. The deposits in Dabola, prospected by the Péchiney Company during the 1940s, offers the advantage of lying along the flanks of valley that is crossed by the road and the railway, faced across the valley by the magnificent waterfalls of Tinkisso, that thus, unites in one place the ore, the electric energy to process it, and the means of shipping it out. As its name, the Futa Jallon suggests that the Futa is the domain of the Fula and of the Jallonké, these latter kin to the Maninka. There are also groups of Coniagui, Bassari, and Tyapi (Cocoli) settled in the north in the region of Youkounkoun and Koundara, along with Diakhanké. The Diakhanké are kin to the Muslims of Baté, sharing a Soninké origin, and are thoroughly Islamized; many of them live in Touba, in the *Cercle* of Gaoual.

South-east of the Futa stretches Upper Guinea, also termed the Manding Plateau. This vast region matches the landscape and the climate of Sudanese areas (i.e., dryer than the Futa), and encloses the basin in which the Niger and its affluents, such as the Milo, shape their courses. It offers many broad alluvial plains, interspersed with marshes, and surrounded by hills worn down by erosion. It offers all the necessary conditions for a variety of agricultural activities, outside its long and hard months of the dry season. The dry season suggests that on average, the region has less precipitation than the Forest Zone to the south or Maritime Guinea. Upper Guinea also has areas that are host to onchocerciasis, an endemic disease also known as river blindness, transmitted through aquatic larvae and flies; the disease causes lesions in the eyes that may lead to blindness.

The local communities engage in raising livestock and in farming a variety of cereal crops and fruits, and specifically, in growing rice. Rice production benefits from the agricultural trials performed at the Bordo Agricultural Center in the suburbs of Kankan, and at the center for mechanized agriculture in Siguiri. In 1958, the expansion of agricultural projects in Upper Guinea, along with those in Maritime Guinea, offered the hope that Guinea might become the "rice-basket" for French-West Africa.

Other features of Upper Guinea include the existence of a variety of ores. There is iron, as everywhere else in Guinea, and bauxite (a sizeable deposit has been noted between the town of Kouroussa and the Tinkisso area). The area is famous for its precious deposits of gold and diamonds. In the 1950s, African goldminers were exploiting alluvial deposits with ancient methods going back to the period of the great medieval empires—the methods that made the savannas of west Africa an El Dorado long before the discovery of the Americas. A modern industrial company is tapping the gold-bearing sands of the Tinkisso by dredging. Guinea's future as a major producer of gold rests on the development of the veins of gold discovered throughout the Niandan-Banié hills in the *Cercles* of Kankan and Kouroussa and around Siguiri. Furthermore, at the edges of Upper Guinea and the Forest Zone, in the district of Kérouané, diamond-mining throughout all the Forest Zone, led, after 1955, to a surge in commercial activity throughout the region, and Kankan in particular. This boom led to a diamond-rush to the mines. The phenomenon increased social divisions in the town, with a visible split between the long-established residents and the diamond-hunters, who had become new landowners and for the most part, were linked with the PDG.

Guinée forestière (Forested Guinea), the fourth natural region, recalls the Futa and Lower Guinea. It offers very hilly terrain, with massifs and small chains of rises, with constant and abundant rainfall and with cool, moist temperatures. The climate gifts the region with special agricultural potential for the large-scale production of high-quality vegetables and citrus fruits. However, difficulties in transportation hinder the marketing of these products. The great stretches of tropical forest, such as those of Diécké, Zima, Guéckédougou, of Kissidougou, of Lola and N'Zérékoré, allow the exploitation of timber in the sawmills that, in large part, belong to the Catholic missions.

The areas peopled by the Kissi are known for their rice-growing, as was noted in 1954 by the ethnologist, Denise Paulme, in her monograph, *Les gens du riz* (the Rice People). Starting in the early 1950s, the principal cash crops were indisputably Robusta coffee, pineapples, and oil-palms, and their rise was linked to the improvement of the roads (to Kankan and Conakry in Guinea, and south to Liberia and Côte d'Ivoire), and to the establishment of a price-stabilization fund. Besides its agricultural potential, the Forest Zone offers rich industrial assets. The rivers, with a full and regular flow, could supply hydro-electric energy. In mineral wealth, geologists readily compared it to the Katanga and Zambian plateau in central Africa. It held iron deposits in Nimba and Simandou, along with reserves of gold, diamonds, and other precious stones. In 1957, studies were underway to devise means to exploit the iron reserves, and thus, to increase the opportunities for development.

Unlike the other regions, each dominated by a majority ethnic group, the Forest Zone is an ethnologic mosaic, home to peoples speaking different languages but sharing some traits. Islam reached the area in the 18TH century, if not earlier, but traditional spirituality persist there, and the "new faith" of Christianity is spreading. The regions face, with some urgency, problems of religious diversity because of the opposition between Christian and Muslims.

We should dwell on the enormous potential of this region. It, by itself, could ensure the needs of the territory. Almost everywhere, people engage in rice-growing, and raise fruits and citrus near the villages or further off in the fields. From Kissidougou to Diendé-Millimono, to Guécké-dougou and to Nongoa on the border with Sierra Leone (and not far from Liberia), the Kissi, the Lélé, and other peoples farm and produce everything: rice, various root-crops, bananas, avocado, and palm-nuts. In the Konya region around the hills of Beyla and the valleys of Sinko, in a world long marked by Islam and regional trade, merchants and consumers together appreciate the value of a rice variety with long and flavored grains. In the sphere of the Toma (or Loma) and the Toma-Manian (of Mande origin), Macenta, with its heights and lowlands, exhibits an ancient tradition of artisanal work along with a mix of crops that includes palm-nuts. From N'Zérékoré to Lola, beyond the mysterious and impressive Mt. Nimba—where, in 1898, the Almami Samory rallied his troops for the last time in their struggle against the white invader—the Guerzé (or Kpellé) also practice diverse agricultural activities, including the production of rice and palm-oil. In short, the rich Forest Zone represents a great asset for the future of Guinea.

After the French conquest in the 1890s, the region became the theater of fierce resistance to the colonial administration. The sacred forests served as strategic places, and even as headquarters. Once the insurrections had been defeated and put down, the Forest Zone opened, bit by bit, to Christianity, brought by the *Pères blancs* (White Fathers), during the first decades of colonization. Slowly, it transformed into a land of coexistence among the spiritual traditions of old Guinea, the Arab-Maninka-Fula world of Islam, and the Judeo-Christianity of western Europe. French schooling hastened the transformation of the region, and enabled it to play a role, along with the three other regions, in the emancipation of the whole territory. The elected representatives of the region, including Sékou Touré, Territorial Councilor for Beyla in 1953, became more and more involved in the Guinean debates.

Such a fabulous catalog of the natural resources of Guinea inspires dreams. Sékou Touré frequently referred to it in his meetings. Such considerations carry weight in politics. At any rate, for 1958, we may speak of Guinea as a coherent and united whole, thanks to the combined effects of colonial administrative actions, the means of communication, the interregional commerce, and of the two World Wars, in which thousands of Guineans saw military service. This combination of factors reinforced a spirit of solidarity that transcended ethnic or religious identity. It brought forth the idea of unity, of a national community, whose members shared a stake in their history and in their natural resources.

Economic and social historic forces, mixed with the integrative powers of religion, acted both as a leaven and as a mortar throughout the ethnic groups and the social strata. Nothing serves better to demonstrate this pluri-ethnic nature than the composition of the two great political groupings, the PDG (*Parti démocratique guinéen*) and the BAG (*Bloc africain de Guinée*), a division that still marks most of the population, despite the overwhelming victory of the PDG in 1957.

At the roots of these two parties, we find activists from all four regions who were welcomed everywhere outside their native regions as fellow citizens. Need we recall that in 1945, Mamba Sano, from the forest, and Yacine Diallo, from the Futa Jallon, were working in the forest when they sought to become *députés* in the National Assembly in Paris? That they were at first even more popular in Kankan than Lamine Sadji Kaba, a native son? Did not Diawandou Barry from the Futa in 1956 win out in Upper Guinea over Sékou Touré?

In 1958, a new nation was in gestation, despite moments of violence that erupted in the cities, which were more a sign of the methods of political mobilization. There were socio-economical divisions. However, the political leader generally guided the divergent forces of the country into a convergent stream. Thus, for example, the competition between Islam and Christianity, in the Maritime and Forest Zones, rarely degenerated into religious struggles. Each political party could take pride in appealing as much to Muslims as to Christians.

The same applied to the opposition of rich and poor or to the contrast of aristocrats (the free-born) and the casted groups (or serfs) that still marked the society in the regions of Moréya, in Maritime Guinea, in the Futa, and in Upper Guinea. Both major parties recruited members, with some success, across all the ethnic groups and all the social strata. All the leaders took satisfaction in the point that Guineans collaborated and worked together without considerations of ethnicity, language, faith, or social origin. We might recall Saïfoulaye Diallo, Louis Lansana Béavogui, and Nyamakoron Kaba, a housewife, and Mamadi Kaba, famous leaders of the PDG and all born to princely clans, who strove for the emancipation of their former serfs.

In that year of 1958, Guinea offered the picture of a land full of promise. It possessed abundant natural resources, a hard-working populace, and dynamic leaders. However, as was observed in 1947 by the visitor Emmanuel Mounier, a noted Christian thinker of the Personalist school (as distinguished from the then-current existentialism), Guinea also seemed to be a "princess who had been abandoned, forgotten by financial capital, and left to slumber in a provincial sweetness."[1]

The traces of this indifference on the part of the federal authorities in Dakar and in the Metropolis in France were still felt, despite significant infrastructure projects launched in the years 1950-1957, such as the paving of the highway axis from Conakry to Kindia and from Conakry to Forécariah; the construction of numerous permanent bridges along the roads of the interior; the extension of the port of Conakry; the development of a port in Benty, on the estuary of the Mellacoré river, to serve the banana plantations; the dredging of the Niger and the Milo rivers to ensure river transport between Bamako in the Soudan (Mali) and Kankan. Still, Emmanuel Mounier had raised the essential and critical point: Guinea required colossal capital investment to bring about mod-

---

1. Emmanuel Mounier, *Oeuvres* (Paris: Seuil, 1962), 3: 323.

ern development. The means of communication in Guinea truly remained archaic. The rainy season rendered the roads impassable; the railway from Conakry to Kankan, intended to unlock access to the interior, was proving to be old and no longer profitable. Thus, Guinea seemed a vast ensemble of public work projects, which alas, were very slow to be launched. The long period of neglect it has suffered might explain the radicalization of the nationalist tendency. The growth of the mining industry, accompanied by the growth in the labor movement, further enhanced this process of radicalization. The lack of progress in the country, no doubt, had some influence on the position of the leaders toward the Referendum.

Another sign of the lack of progress was the preponderance of the local trade. The economy of Guinea was dominated by the great French trading companies, with the Greek businesses and the Lebano-Syrian shops.[2] Devoted entirely to the export-import trade, these companies invested very little in industry, channeling all profits out of the country. This local commerce relegated African merchants to retail sales at the lowest level, with minimal access to bank loans. The development of an African bourgeoisie was thus retarded, and this fact led to undesirable consequences, for the lack of capital and the absence of modern entrepreneurs constitute a void that it is difficult to fill.

The challenge facing Guinea was to produce new women and men for an efficient economy. While impressive, the mining industry also presented problems. In the years 1952-58, it experienced increasing growth, which led to the creation of many jobs through the Mining Company of Conakry, at the bauxite deposits from Kassa to the Loos Islands, to the deposits in Fria, and even those in Boké, which were still in the exploration and planning stages, as well as the gold and diamond mines in the interior. In 1958, Guinea offered no true industries besides the plants that produced fruit juices and carbonated beverages and the plastics factory in the suburbs of Conakry, owned by a Lebanese, Albert Constantin, who lived in Beyla and Kankan beforehand. The mines, in short, were far from

---

2. Among the principal commercial companies were the CFAO (*Compagnie française de l'Afrique occidentale*), SCOA (*Société commericale de l'ouest Africain*), the Compagnie du Niger français, the Compagnie Peyrissac, UNICOMER (*Union commerciale d'outre-mer*), CCFA (*Comptoir commercial franco-africain*), SIAG (*Société industrielle et automotive de Guinée*), the English company, PZ (Paterson Zochonis), and the Greek companies, Foufounis and Théodossopoulos.

creating centers of development; they were, rather, a more refined form of the local trade economy.

The same observation about the lack of progress would apply to the development of hydro-electric energy. As early as 1952, the dam at the *Grandes Chutes* (Great Falls) between Kindia and Conakry supplied the capital with electricity. The authorities were prospecting the immense hydro-electric potential of the basin of the Konkouré river; the plans envisioned the creation of several dams/factories that might supply all the electrical needs of the country and of neighboring territories. In 1957, a general inventory of equipment and of challenges had been completed, and the phase of construction was planned for the end of 1958. The Konkouré project was intended to create the impetus required for the industrialization of Guinea, to ensure its future, and to make it the industrial center of West Africa.

Given the number of development projects in Guinea, it seemed fair to wonder if a negative vote in the Referendum might not preclude their fulfillment.[3] Would the International Bank for Reconstruction and Development (IBRD) and private funding organizations be willing to advance funds to a new Guinean state without sanction from France? Furthermore, what might come of the 200 billion Metropolitan Francs that were being invested? The Referendum on September 28 would determine the question.

The results of the Referendum in Guinea are thus to be understood considering the consequences of its delayed economic development and the effects of the mobilization of social forces composed of youth groups, students, women, labor unions, and religious movements. These conditions presented a different character to political activity from that found in the other territories of the A.O.F. The struggle of the parties there seemed a microcosm of the awakening throughout Francophone West Africa. The country was familiar with issues ranging from labor unions to traditional chiefdoms and to religious brotherhoods.

The labor movement carried more weight than elsewhere. The triumph of the PDG was inseparable from the labor unrest, especially after the great strike of 1953. The PDG had brought forth the USTG (*Union des syndicats des travailleurs de Guinée*: United Unions of the Workers of

---

3. See Philippe Decraene, *Le Monde* for September 27, 1958.

Guinea), that included all the unions except that of the teachers and the railway workers. Sékou Touré had assigned to himself the task of integrating into society this new stratum of wage-earners, proletarians, and semi-proletarians, through improvement in their working conditions.

In 1958, there was yet no unity in the labor movement. Railway workers and teachers opposed each other in the USTG headquarters. They were hostile to the constitutional framework and spoke out in favor of independence. They denounced the collusion between the PDG and the colonial authority. The Teachers' Union deserves special attention. Koumandian Kéita, the Secretary General and an influential member of the BAG, counted among the virulent critics of Sékou Touré. At the Convention of 1957, held in Mamou, Kéita threatened the government with a general strike. Teachers were a real force at the heart of the PDG. Samba Lamine Traoré, Mountaga Baldé, Fatou Aribot, and Bah-Ibrahima Kaba constituted the left wing, meaning the intellectual branch of the party, sharing views close to the platform of the PAI (*Parti africain de l'indépendence:* African Independence Party). Since the end of the Second World War, there had been an expansion in educational efforts. The curriculum had been brought up to date, and a variety of secondary and primary schools had been established. However, much still needed to be done in this critical area. By Touré's count, the number of Guineans who had completed the *cycle supérieur* (advanced courses) at the University of Dakar or in France was tallied only in dozens![4]

Students left their mark upon the youth and the wider population through their knowledge and their artistic and sporting activities during the vacations, and further, through their political involvement. In the cities, cultural centers encouraged the arts and the participation of young women. The students also competed in sporting events in urban stadiums, in artistic competitions, and in political debates held at the centers; they thus contributed to the emergence of a Guinean self-awareness. The Bérété Brothers, Charles Diané, Ibrahima Kaké, Sékou Traoré, and Cheikh Chérif, all stressed, and for good cause, the political role of the students.[5] They were activists within the UGEG (*Union générale des étudiants guinéens:* General Union of Students of Guinea), which was the

---

4. Sékou Touré, "IVe Congrès dui PDG" in *L'expérience guinéenne*, 61.
5. Kaké, *op. cit.*; Sékou Traoré, *Les documents de la FEANF* (Paris: Harmattan, 1986).

regional chapter of the FEANF (*Fédération des étudiants d'Afrique noire en France*: Federation of Students from Black Africa in France). They had already, in July of 1957, during the Convention of Conakry, criticized the general achievements of Sékou Touré's government, in concert with the Teachers' Union and youth groups; they then spoke out for independence. In 1958, a strike by the students at the *École normale de Kindia* (the Teacher-training School of Kindia), which led Sékou Touré to close the establishment immediately, marked a further step in the radicalization of the students and the teachers. In their Convention, held in July of 1958, the students started their campaign for a "NO" vote at the Referendum, even before the events of August 25 TH. Guinea's response to General de Gaulle is to be understood not only in the light of the impact of movements from labor leaders and students, but also in terms of women's movements and religious movements. The PDG was leading a struggle against the survival of forms of exploitation and oppression of women and people of caste or of servile origin. The party was opposed to forms of inequality.

Women counted among the first groups to grasp the revolutionary language of the PDG and to organize for its success. They were the spearheads, and they attacked the fortresses of the opposition and invigorated the activities of local chapters. The names of M'Balia Camara, of Fatou Aribot, and of Maffory Bangoura in Lower Guinea; of Nénéfouta Baldé, Hadja Bobo Diallo, and Kadiatou Pété Baldé in Middle Guinea; of Nyamakoron Kaba and Gbélia-Diéné Camara in Kankan; of Loffo Camara and Djédoua Diabaté-Kourouma in the Forest Zone: all should be written down as part of the epic of women working for the PDG/RDA. The Organization of Women within the PDG led the government to adopt a plan for women's emancipation.

The PDG denounced the traditional system of aristocracy. In so doing, it benefited from the issues posed by the former serfs or casted persons throughout the regions: in the Susu area of Moréah, and among the Fula of the Futa and the Malinké of Upper Guinea. The issue allowed the party expansion into those regions. In the Futa, where notions of servitude and ethnic prejudice survived, the PDG, acting through Saïfoulaye Diallo and his colleagues of noble origin, promoted a spirit of equality. Diallo urged a reform of the agrarian system and the establishment of democracy at the village level. To achieve these goals, the party presented candidates, all over the territory, drawn from the under-privileged classes. This policy allowed the party to take root in the villages at the expense of the BAG. All this influenced the results of the Referendum. Religious issues also played to the advantage of the PDG. Guinean society had a profound respect for religion. People revered Islam, Christianity, and the local spiritual traditions. Politics and religion were intermixed. It was the support of Muslim notables that contributed to the success of the BAG, up until 1957. The PDG's strategy was to challenge the spiritual foundations of the authority of the marabouts, along with the collusion between colonialism and the Catholic church, and to claim a theology almost of liberation.

In general practice, the previous Catholic establishment, led by the Mgr. Lerouge and later by Mgr. de Milleville, had opposed the PDG because of its Marxist tendencies. The priests, and especially the *Pères blancs* and the *Congrégation du saint-esprit* (Congregation of the Holy Spirit) denounced the PDG and threatened its members and sympathizers with excommunication. This was a continuation of a struggle against materialism. The colonial administration, while laic, was reluctant to promote African clergy in the hierarchy. These factors led the PDG to describe the church as a "regressive institution." The problem was more complex. Many Christian activists, particularly in the Forest Zone and along the coast, were working for the party. In the districts of Maritime Guinea and the Forest, the Catholic church represented a force that the party could not ignore. Thus, both sides faced the need to establish some common ground.

Within the Catholic church, changes were underway, impelled by the actions of young priests open to new ideas. Among them, we should note the Fathers Gérard Vieira and Eugene Creuse Berger, who were teachers in the seminary that later became the private secondary school of Dixinn. Father Vieira, a French priest of the Congregation of the Holy Spirit, through his exceptional abilities as a teacher and an organizer of the youth, through his broad-mindedness, his kindness, and his profound respect for other religious values, left his mark not only on the faithful but also on a generation of Catholic and Muslim students. He later worked in Dakar, before returning to France where he died. Through his work emerged the conviction that the church, far from fettering change, should embody the values of freedom and of love to create the "City of God." The faith, in this view, must engage with history, with the present, and with all its contradictions and hopes.

Moreover, the African clergy—their spokesman was Father Raymond-Marie Tchidimbo, later to become Archbishop of Conakry—saw no opposition between Christianity and African emancipation. Father Tchidimbo was considered a troublemaker by some of his European colleagues; he maintained a dialogue with the leaders of the PDG, and he presented himself as the vicar to the Catholic flock that also belonged to the Party. This new category of priests imbued the Church with the image of progress and liberation. The Christian community of Guinea, therefore, responded to the appeal of the parties for the vote on September 28TH.

The same urge to turn religious faith into a motive for political action affected a certain category of Muslims. They felt that it was a matter of recognizing, in Islam, its call as a religion of progress and liberty, and to help the country free itself from the lordship of the colonizers, and also of religious charlatans. This position required a struggle against the marabouts allied with the traditional oligarchy. Many leaders of the PDG profited from the propagation of the fundamentalist doctrine, termed Wahhabist or *soubanoun* in Maninka, that entered Upper Guinea through the ever-increasing influence of the pilgrimage to Mecca and through the teachings of graduates of the Arabic universities of Kairouan (in Tunisia), and particularly, of Al-Azhar in Cairo.[6] These graduates had been active in Bamako since 1946. Why did the Wahhabists challenge the marabouts?

The Wahhabists denounced the mystic/magical arsenal of the local spirituality (such as divination), performed by some marabouts within Islamic rituals. They also criticized the "healer-marabouts and the readers of sand and cowries" as exploiting the credulity of the peoples. They denounced the allies of the BAG who profited from these practices. They even took issue with certain great marabouts who encouraged veneration of the divinities.

Such debates on theological matters can arouse great passion. Communities split into factions: reformist or traditional. The reformist camp

---

6. Roland Pré, *L'avenir de la Guinée* (Conakry : Editions guinéennes, 1951), 24-25, 47, 51.

will attract young members—in this case, mostly traders and long-haul transporters, who had been exposed to the RDA for some time and followed a doctrine that promoted individual responsibility and freedom. Meanwhile, the older doyens and the notables hold to the Islam of the elders and the marabouts. The anti-colonialism of the Wahhabists made them natural allies of the PDG. Many party leaders followed the fundamentalist doctrine: Dr. El-Hadj Abdoulaye Touré, a member of the governing committee of Kankan and later, the Minister for Foreign Affairs; El-Hadj Aboubakar Diallo (of Kankan), Chief of Cabinet in the Ministry of Public Works; Youssouf Nabaniou Chérif, a political official in Boké and later, the Secretary General of the Chapter in Conakry. Sékou Touré himself showed interest in the movement, to some extent. The fundamentalist leaders of Guinea were active in favor of the Federal Executive and the unity of the A.O.F. They offered criticism of Houphouët-Boigny and his "policy of Balkanization," while corresponding with their colleagues in other territories.

Sékou Touré in discussion with Senegalese politician figures, ca. 1960. Photo by Karim Ndiaye

This movement gave rise to the Convention of Dakar in December 1957, which endowed the Senegalese Association known as the *Union culturelle musulmane* (UCM: Muslim Cultural Union) with a West African presence. A large contingent of Guineans attended the Convention. Among the leaders to be seen there were figures mentioned above: Dr. Abdoulaye Touré, Aboubakar Diallo, and Youssouf Nabaniou. There were also merchants, such as El-Hadj Fa Sylla and El-Hadj Damanda-Fodé Cissé; Arabic-speaking scholars, such as El-Hadj Kabiné Diané, former imam of Bouaké in Côte d'Ivoire, famous for having translated the Qur'ān, El-Hadj Mohamed Fodé Kéita, both of them founders of the Wahhabist School in Bamako, and Fodé Souleymane Kanté, a schoolmaster, and all of them linked with the RDA.

In 1958, the Guinean branches collaborated with chapters of the PDG. This experience demonstrates that religion and politics are not incompatible. As we were told by Dr. El-Hadj Abdoulaye Touré, during an interview in New York in 1970—he was then the Guinean Ambassador to the United Nations—that, "Nothing could be more natural than the inspiration drawn by the PDG from Islam! Muslim values have long been part of the cultural foundations of Guinea. And the Party understands the necessity of aligning their policies and their activities with the great liberating ideals of Islam." This process continued until the Referendum.

In 1958, Guinea was living under the regime of the "Loi-cadre ou Loi Defferre," and under the administration of the PDG. In the elections of 1957, the opposition had been crushed and its chiefs humiliated. The Administration aimed to eliminate the opposition and establish a single-party system. When the PDG held its convention in January of 1958, Touré, in fact, invited the "brothers of the BAG and the socialists to learn the lesson of the events, and to make up their minds to join the ranks of the Party of the people of Guinea."[7] Unification did not take place, although there were defections, particularly among members of the civil service and among businessmen. The violence, however, proved unsettling.

The campaigns of intimidation at the start of 1958, and especially the heated clashes that caused bloodshed in Conakry on May 2ND, were intended to weaken and uproot the opposition. The eruption of such violence in April and May of 1958 was difficult to explain, since Touré was ruling "as governor," as the songs went. The upheavals, however, were a continuation of a tradition that tied political awaking to tinges of eth-

---

7. Sékou Touré, "Assises du PDG" in *L'expérience guinéenne*, 31.

nicity. The Fula were assumed to be anti-PDG, "saboteurs." This view had held since the strike of November 1953; the strike's success enhanced the aureole around Sékou Touré's movement. These conflicts were termed the "*Kinnsi* wars" (Kinnsi in Susu is a plant used to create protective hedges). They had many victims and caused much damage; they also led to the exile of many families, only a few months before independence. The PDG, ruling the administration, wished to draw up a slate of its goals, looking ahead to the next elections. Their program included: liberation of political detainees; abolition of traditional chieftaincy; recruitment through competitive examination of new administrative agents; an increase in salaries and in family allowances; reduction of the personal tax; defense of womens' rights, and reduction of dowries; encouraging female education; eliminating the monopoly on rice held by the large companies; the creation of a stabilization fund for crops such as bananas, coffee, and cocoa; and the deregulation of diamond-mining.

This program further increased Touré's popularity. The Party convention allowed him the opportunity to express his reservations about the "Loi-cadre" and to demand complete internal autonomy, along with other reforms that stipulated an ever-increasing transfer of powers. Slowly, a consensus on these issues was emerging in Guinea. Everything created the conditions that favored a vote of "NO" in the Referendum of September 28.

CHAPTER 5
"NO" TO DE GAULLE, "YES" TO INDEPENDENCE

WE RETURN TO the morning of August 26, 1958. General de Gaulle offers his best wishes to Guinea, and his airplane takes off from the airport in Gbessia. On the way back, in the car carrying them into Conakry, Sékou Touré, President of the Territorial Council, and Governor Jean Mauberna conversed.

"Why did you offend the General in that way?" asked Mauberna.

"What did I say that isn't general knowledge?" answered Touré. "My speech was just what I have been saying for months—you know that better than anyone."

"But the tone was too harsh, toward an elder, a famous man, who was your guest."[1]

To those comments, that contained a bitter criticism bearing on the rules of civility, Sékou Touré was at a loss for an answer. He remained pensive, perhaps worried. Did he regret the verbal violence of the previous evening? Had he mistaken the situation? Didn't the speech match his political views? Wasn't he sincere? Who knows? But what to make of the thin-skinned reaction on the part of the General? These questions absorbed him until he got back to his office. There, he was awaited by many party leaders who had come to attend the welcome to General de Gaulle and were there to congratulate him and to ask questions. They held a meeting for clarification, in which Touré restated the positions of

---

1. Lacouture, *Cinq hommes et la France*, 353.

Guinea and announced that he planned to take the next plane to Dakar to renew contact with political and labor leaders. Thereupon, he learned from Governor Mauberna that a plane, provided by Cornut-Gentille, waited to take him to Dakar. Despite some hesitations, he took it, and that evening, arrived in the capital of the A.O.F.

In Dakar, Touré learned that Senghor, Mamadou Dia (Chair of the Governing Council), and Lamine Guèye (Leader of the Assembly) were all absent, and that the General had been treated to a stormy welcome. The atmosphere in the city was very tense. Late that evening, he, once again, discussed the referendum with Cornut-Gentille, the Minister for Overseas France. Sékou Touré was keenly conscious of Cornut-Gentille's regard for him. However, he wished to be known as a man of principles. Thus, he reassured the French minister of his attachment to the plans for a Franco-African Community. He wished that General de Gaulle might grasp the merit of the claims put forth by Guinea, which, in short, meant that there had to be a mention, in the text of the constitution, of the existence of an independent A.O.F., with its own independent Federal Executive, as a prerequisite for any association with France. As he, Touré, saw it, these claims in no way echoed anti-French sentiment; to the contrary, their purpose was to endow Franco-African relations with new meaning, more in accord with the deep aspirations of most Africans—and, one might say, one that conformed with the former French policy of centralization, and the present orientation of her own African policy. Sily hoped that the former High-Commissioner of the A.O.F. could report these views to the General, with whom he also would like to talk.

However, the General was not available. Touré had forgotten that the General detested prevarication, and that Cornut-Gentille was losing influence in the immediate circle of the General. The General's clear and definite position could be defined in these terms: Community with France, as stipulated in the text of the draft constitution; there remained a possibility that territories might form groups if they so wished (but the Metropolis would not grant institutional status). Thus, the attempt at mediation by the Minister for Overseas France proved, once again, a failure. On August 27, General de Gaulle ended his African visit. That morning, his plane took off for Algiers—whose problems had, in fact, led to his return to power. Still, he left Cornut-Gentille behind in Dakar. He, indefatigable, took advantage of this stay to renew, again, his discussions with the man from Conakry. For all told, the question irritated him. During the night of August 27-28TH, Cornut-Gentille and Sékou Touré conversed at length. The discussions were not easy, for since Conakry, the situation was becoming ever more complex with each passing day, and the Guinean leader was chary. So, the Minister for Overseas France employed all his dexterity to reassure his counterpart, and thus, to achieve his ends. So, it is reported in the circles close to Touré.

The Minister felt that he knew Sily, and that he was susceptible to praise. And so, speaking from the start as a former Governor General, he said that he understood why large groupings were necessary in the past colonial context and given present geo-politics. He saw great worth in Federalism. However, speaking as a pragmatist, the Minister invited Sékou Touré to recall the debates of the Constitutional Consultative Committee, and to realize that it was too late to consider new proposals. In his opinion, Touré had given proof of a great pragmatism when he agreed to present the perspective of the RDA to the General on August 5, despite his own reservations. He felt that this same pragmatism should guide the choice of Guinea in the matter of the referendum. And then later, Guinea, along with all the territories that might choose so, could collaborate in establishing a Federal unit associated with France. As Cornut-Gentille saw the matter, this was the wise solution that would also maintain Franco-Guinea amity, as de Gaulle perceived it, and that would be beneficial for Guinea.

Sékou Touré did not see the matters in these terms. He found it difficult to understand why the A.O.F. should be dismantled right then, when it would be so easy to preserve it. To this most pertinent question, the former High-Commissioner reminded the Deputy Mayor of Conakry that the A.O.F. was a colonial creation that certain territorial leaders were now rejecting. Consequently, he added, it was now the business of Africans to determine their own conditions aiming toward a Federal association. Sékou Touré demanded that the French government maintain the institution that had already proved its worth. Since the Minister could not assure such an outcome, the conversation turned to another strategy.

The Minister changed his tactics and hoped to sway Sékou Touré by addressing economic questions. As a former Governor, he knew that Guineans placed enormous importance on the development of their country, blessed with abundant natural resources, and that they expected their government to provide concrete results in that sphere. The Minister renewed his comments on the colossal financial investments required to launch the giant projects in Guinea that the France of de Gaulle was ready to encourage and ensure on good financial terms. These projects affected all the sectors of the economy, and they would establish the prestige and the prosperity of Guinea.

Basically, the French Minister was appealing to the common sense of the leader of the PDG and evoking his responsibilities as a leader in the struggle against under-development and poverty. The French government saw economic collaboration as an essential element in Franco-African friendship, and that collaboration depended on politics. De Gaulle was counting on victory in the referendum. For all these reasons, Cornut-Gentille hoped that Sékou Touré would follow in the path of the RDA to bring about a vote for "Yes." Thus, politics serves economic interest, for which the leader can take credit before his people. Didn't this make sense?

The leader from Conakry reflected for a moment. Answering, he stressed that he was attached to Franco-Guinean friendship. He felt, however, that the referendum was only a vote on a proposed set of laws, and that in no way should it affect relations or investments, since Guinea wished to remain associated with France. Touré found it hard to grasp the necessity that General de Gaulle had created between a "Yes" vote and French assistance. He rejected pressures and menaces, and demanded, once again, that the government add the creation of a Federal Executive into the final text of the constitution. Thereupon, the Minister for Overseas France accepted the facts: he had been mistaken on the character of the Guinean leader. Touré was proving himself an intransigent idealist, stung by the barb of cultural nationalism and fanatical. Late that night, the discussions ended.

His stay in Dakar provided Sékou Touré the opportunity to discuss the organization of a "common front" with his comrades from the UGTAN (*Union générale des travailleurs de l'Afrique noire*: General Union of Workers of Black Africa) and Bakary Djibo, head of the government of Niger, who had come to meet General de Gaulle. To some extent, he was successful, for his counterpart from Niger and Abdoulaye Diallo, Minister of Labor for the Soudan (Mali), joined him on a radio program for a thunderous set of speeches that confirmed their cultural nationalism.

The substance of Touré's position was this: Given the choice of voting "Yes" for a constitution that would debase the dignity, the freedom, and the unity of Africa, or accepting, as General de Gaulle had put it forth, immediate independence, Guinea would unhesitatingly choose independence. We shall not yield to extortion by France; we could not accept menaces or pressures aimed at our lands to choose—against all our feelings and our understanding—the conditions of a marriage that would retain us in the complex of the colonial administration.... We speak for a "No"—unanimous and definite—for any proposal that deviates from these choices." Through the speech, broadcast on the radio, and through the resurgence of his nationalist tendency, Touré aligned himself with the "No." The decision had been made.

On his return to Conakry, Sily held a gigantic meeting in the Vox Cinema during the afternoon of August 28. Facing the activists of his party, he restated his arguments, dwelling more on the problems with the proposed legislation than on the advantages. He stressed the point that to some extent, the proposed legislation lagged the current legal framework. The problems included the obligation for Africans to vote at once for both their fate and to establish a constitution, while they would no longer be represented in the French National Assembly; the common holding of natural resources, and France's control over the economies of African territories; the barriers to African engagement with other countries; and finally, the threats of secession and sanction in the case of a negative vote. The Secretary General of the PDG concluded: "Our choice is in favor of France; it would never be against France.... It is the choice of the government of France to answer 'YES' or 'NO' to aspirations toward the unity of Africa. But should the government of France prove unwilling to offer equal respect to the dignity of Africa, we will say 'YES' to France, but we shall say 'NO' to the government, 'NO' to the constitution."[2] The Hall broke out in applause.

Touré was aware of the currents of agitation that swept the European community in Guinea after the visit of General de Gaulle. On August 29, Touré accepted the invitation from Auguste Pouech, Chair of the Chamber of Commerce of Conakry, to "offer all the necessary explanations"

---

2. Touré, "Conférence publique," *op cit.*, 103. See also, "Discours à la Chambre de commerce," 145.

and to reassure the business sector. After an extensive and emotional historical lecture, he proclaimed that Guinea's membership "remained conditional on respect for unity." And he added, as a conclusion, "We will take no position on secession from France; it may be granted, but we do not desire it. We shall vote against the proposal, and we shall tell France: "We wish to remain linked with you on such and such terms." We also know that the interests not only of Guinea are to be considered, but also those of France. Secession will be avoided because, for the whole territory, we shall have found the basis for an association that respects reciprocal interest."

Finally, Touré assured the French of Conakry that everything would happen quietly, because of the engagement and the discipline of the people. It was clear that the die had been cast. Sékou Touré's strategy, henceforth, consisted in fidelity to his principles of African dignity and unity, while also seeking out the means for close collaboration with France in a new understanding.

Obviously, in the high political spheres of Paris, people continued to wonder about Guinea. It was also noted that Cornut-Gentille had far less influence on Sékou Touré than had been believed. De Gaulle, therefore, opposed Cornut-Gentille's desire to return to Guinea; he preferred to leave matters in the hands of Houphouët-Boigny. Houphouët could number among his assets his position as President of the RDA and the assistance of Ouezzin Coulibaly, whose influence on Sékou Touré was undeniable.

However, through one of those ironies of fate, Ouezzin was just then admitted to a hospital in Paris due to falling seriously ill. Consequently, the meeting of the Coordinating Committee, the highest authority of the RDA, that had been planned for September 4 in Ouagadougou, had to be cancelled. Instead, a meeting of the members of the Political Bureau was called and was to be held at the bedside of Ouezzin Coulibaly in Paris. Sékou Touré refused to attend because of his opposition to a communiqué issued on August 31, signed by the hand of Coulibaly, that criticized the statements made by the leader of the PDG on August 27 and 28. At the Paris meeting of the RDA representatives, Bengaly Camara, Minister for Labor, and Dr. Najib Roger Accar, Minister of Health, represented Guinea: but, they did not participate in the discussions. "The RDA was satisfied with the constitutional proposal," was the conclusion, and they opted for a "YES."

On September 7, Ouezzin Coulibaly died of liver cancer. To general surprise, Sékou Touré did not attend the funeral ceremonies held on September 15 in Bobo-Dioulasso. The absence of the Guinean leader was a shock to the feelings of the Party leaders. First, it was a terrible transgression, and it ran counter to African customs. Second, it showed flagrant disloyalty to the Party that had done so much for him, and a lack of solidarity with his companions in the struggle. The leaders of the RDA and Houphouët-Boigny were henceforth convinced that Sékou Touré wished to ride alone. Nevertheless, they engaged in some last-minute initiatives to bring the PDG back into alignment with the larger RDA.

Without any further equivocation, Touré laid out in detail his thoughts and his position in a public declaration. His speech on September 12 officially opened the electoral campaign. In that speech, he restated his criticisms about the constitutional proposal, he invited the people to maintain order and discipline, and he called for a massive "YES" vote in favor of independence. In tempestuous tones, he threw out the proposition: "To vote 'NO' is to save the cost of a war!" In enraged tones, he offered this statement: "The French should not believe, in present circumstances, that the Independence of the Negroes has any relation to the revenge of slaves." This language, lacking all delicacy, left little doubt about his intentions. In closing, he denounced the corruption of money, and the lack of historical consciousness and pride. And, honoring a tradition a resistance and seeking to further justify his position, he placed himself in the line of the great figures who have provided African history with its glorious and noble pages.

Considering the many statements uttered by Sékou Touré following August 9, how can we explain the dialogue he held with Dr. Charles Diané, President of the FEANF (*Fédéraion des étudiants d'Afrique noire en France*: Federation of the Students of Black Africa in France), and other student leaders in Conakry at the start of September? In that conversation, Sékou Touré was still not completely won over to the idea of independence. Here is how Dr. Charles Diané of Kankan reported his words to the historian Ibrahima Kaké:

We proposed, during the drafting of the constitutional proposal, to

*allow for the creation, in Dakar or in Abidjan, of a Federal
Executive branch with a federal government and a federal
Parliament. The Metropolis has offered no concrete answer to this
request so far. This offers us a valid reason for answering 'NO.'
However, it is not only an institutional question. There is also the
question of the capability of exercising state powers, that would be
the consequence of a native vote. Consider Guinea, to speak only
of her. We have no infrastructure, we can't even produce a match,
and far less build factories. That is why we shall follow the
guidance adopted by the Coordinating Committee (of the
RDA).*[3]

The realistic tone of this interview is surprising. Touré was apparently
aware of the difficulties associated with premature and poorly-prepared
independence. He found himself caught on the back foot against isolation and adventurism, in these terms:

*I do not think that Africa is ripe for independence. That is why—
should I receive a firm commitment from General de Gaulle—I
shall ask the people of Guinea to vote 'YES'. I will not hide from
you, moreover, the fact that I have approached persons in the
circle of General de Gaulle and other French notables such as
Mitterand and Mendès France, with the goal of making possible
the creation of an Executive with a Federal Parliament.*

Convinced that he followed correct principles, Sékou Touré offered the
impression that it was the intransigence of de Gaulle over the question of
the Federal Executive that had backed him, Touré, into an uncomfortable
situation, and one that went against "his reason and his heart." This put
him in a bad corner. In short, the disagreement rose from the personalities of the two men. De Gaulle and Touré were both filled with a sense
of honor and status, and both were most stubborn after they had made
their decision. Thereupon, they could remove all stops in service of their
respective goal.

Seen in this way, the intention of voting "YES" or "NO" in Guinea on

---

3. See Kaké, *op.cit.*, 64-68.

September 28 would essentially be an extension of the quarrel—or per-haps better, the opposition—between two strong egos. The constitutional proposal was a thought-out action that for some time, had inspired the passion of the General, and that elicited in Sékou Touré a reaction, no less strong, against some positions taken by the General, reflecting, on Touré's part, the instinctive reaction to maintain the unity of the A.O.F.

For Guinea, and especially for Sékou Touré, the opportunity for some official determination about the referendum came on September 14, the occasion of the territorial conference of the PDG in Conakry. It was also the final opportunity for the ruling wing of the RDA to try a last attempt at repairing the breach that had opened on August 25. The RDA sent two leaders of territorial governments—Gabriel Lisette from Chad and Jean-Marie Koné from the Soudan/Mali—as well as Doudou Guèye, a Senegalese who was Chair of the Permanent Commission of the Great Council. These were important personages, of course, but of somewhat secondary rank. It seemed that the headquarters of the RDA, with cause and already offended by Sékou Touré's absence from the funeral of Ouezzin Coulibaly, viewed his position as a manipulative effort to make them plead with him, and thus, to enhance further his stature. This could certainly explain the absence of the major leaders of the movement in Conakry.

The presence of the three delegates, emissaries to the PDG, had little effect on the Convention. The conference offered the Guinean leader the chance to brush up his philosophical and historical overview of imperi-alism and colonial domination, of African nationalism, and of the polit-ical efforts of the PDG. This was the context in Guinea and the broad panorama throughout the country. Presented as such by speakers all fully engaged with history, the *geste* of the great figures of African resistance to colonial expansion takes a central place in the presentation made at this gathering. A sense of history—a fecund source of inspiration—offered the main speaker, Sékou Touré, an invitation to act boldly in the present. In the name of that history and that honor, he invited the African leaders to follow in the path of the illustrious heroes:

> *Our ancestors fought the French penetration until their army was lost. Our generation will have the historic privilege, of enabling their land to retrieve its full and entire liberty, through the most*

peaceful of means—for it requires only voting no.... Who can
imagine the international repercussions of a unanimous vote by
Africans, rejecting independence in favor of a regime of
depersonalization? Such a result would smother our generation
in indignity and compel its condemnation by future generations.[4]

Sékou Touré saw the referendum as an unhoped-for chance, and the
vote as an effective and powerful weapon against colonial domination.
Equipped with this weapon, political leaders might raise themselves, in
the vision of the leader of Conakry, to the rank of the ancestors, those
"proud warriors" and builders of empire.

That is why, intoxicated by the frenetic crowd, he could state, over-
proudly:

Dear Comrades, it falls to us to preserve the honor of the African,
for Guinea and for Africa. We shall thus achieve a decisive action
in the history of this continent, transforming the land from a
dependency to a free country. We shall therefore vote 'NO' to a
Community that is the same French union under a different
name—old goods under a new label. We shall vote 'NO' to
inequality; we shall be an independent country. The 28TH of
September shall henceforth be our national holiday, and thus,
through a chance that marks our history as a sign, the month of
September that in 1898 was the determining date of the
colonization of Guinea by France, in 1958 September will be the
moment on which independence was granted.[5]

There was no longer any doubt. Sékou Touré was haunted by the deeds
and the figure of Almami Samori, his ancestor, and as we must say, who
was arrested by the French—here is a true coincidence of history—on
September 29, 1898. The decision had been made, and it was irrevocable.

Before loud plaudits, the Convention adopted the directives of its Secretary General, although we do not know by what majority. Following
this action, in conclusion, and perhaps without irony, the head of the

---

4. Sékou Touré, "Conférence territoriale du PDG," *op. cit.,* 179.
5. *Ibid.* 180.

Party paid homage to the French government for its actions. He urged upon all the groups vigilance, to thwart any attempts at provocation and intimidation.

There, under a thatched shelter, unadorned and plain, the representatives of cities and towns from the Atlantic coast to the majestic Mt. Nimba, from the marshy rivers of Soumbouya in Lower Guinea to the vast and grassy plains of Fié in Upper Guinea, those delegates, delirious, spoke out for independence. This popular reaction made September 14, 1958, a memorable date in the history of Guinea. For Sékou Touré, it was truly a "night of August 4"—the night, we might recall, on which the National Assembly of the French Revolution in 1789 abolished privileges and destroyed the *Ancien régime*.

Eyewitnesses, such as Lamine Kaba, nicknamed *Niger*, a former member of the Governing Committee in Kankan, Ismaël Kéita, known as *Gros Bois* (Big Wood), and Mamadi Doumbouya, known as *Magie* (Magic)—both former members of the RDA youth groups in Kankan, and others, allow us to say that September 14 marked the direct intervention of the populace into the debating space over the constitution. Hitherto, the people had been following the discussions, without any concrete participation. Obviously, the political leaders, at every level, regularly offered meetings to explain the positions taken and the course of events. On September 14, the people of Guinea seized control of its destiny. The meeting was preceded by a swarming throng that swept the country to its furthest corners, the very image of the party that dominated political life in the territory. On all sides, along all the thoroughfares, the delegates of all status marched out. They took over the trains and the tramways and the inter-urban buses by assault. All these people were governed by a single idea and a single desire: to reach Conakry and to participate in the Convention. Welcoming committees were set up throughout the city in primary and secondary schools, then in vacation. Townsfolk opened their doors to relatives, to friends, and to strangers. The atmosphere rendered September 14 a date of comparable importance (of course, with necessary qualifiers) to July 14, 1789 (start of the French Revolution). The event was not the movement of a mob against a fortified citadel, but the expression of the force of an entire people in an assault on colonialism and in quest of liberty. Like a people with a single goal, Guinea proclaimed that it was a united and indivisible nation.

Reinforcing this impression, expressions of support poured in through all parts of the territory in the form of telegrams. In unison with the people in attendance, the senders extolled their support for the nation that was to be born. The voices of the leaders of the opposition, even, spoke out in favor of the views of the PDG. Guinea stood out as an islet standing as a single person, sheltered from winds and tides of division, and facing a future whose auguries were unclear. Sékou Touré did not expect the isolation of Guinea. He believed that the governments of Niger and of Senegal might go along with the PDG; the governments there were ruled by the PRA, a party with well-known opposition to the Balkanization of the A.O.F. He was also counting on mass movements organized by the UGTAN and the other labor organizations. However, he was brought back to earthly reality when he met with Mamadou Dia, President of the Council for Senegal, whom Senghor had dispatched to explain, with some embarrassment, their position: they faced business groups, the *grands marabouts* (principal Muslim clerics), and the "underlying people" of Senegal that obliged the leaders to abandon the "NO" that had clearly been expected, in favor of a "YES" that clearly went against logic. Sékou Touré understood this; he was to ride alone as he made his vault into the unknown. He realized then that it was a matter of pride and of dignity.

In truth, as it is told in Conakry, Guineans did not believe there would be economic sanctions or that French technical assistance would be withdrawn. They were persuaded that France would remain involved, and that Touré would be able to negotiate pacts of agreement with the French government. The more so because the major French investors were very interested in the resources of Guinea, and that the French Treasury had noted the surplus in the trade balance, measured in foreign exchange, that Guinea provided. However, time was growing short, and worries were increasing.

In Paris, various notables tried to intervene and prevent a brutal and unnecessary break, but the messages reached Matignon too late. It was no longer possible. From that point on, Conakry became aware of the gravity and the extent of the situation. When Conakry requested the start of negotiations with France, the day after the Referendum, Paris summoned Governor Mauberna and ordered him to leave Guinea. This led to madness in the European community throughout Guinea. The reaction unleashed a huge rush to liquidate properties, to transfer capital, and to suspend transactions. The arrival of a company of paratroopers from Dakar "to reinforce order increased the panic among the Europeans, and intimidated and irritated the Africans." Bit by bit, a general mobilization took place under conditions of order and discipline.

After a few days, Guinea began to act; wisely, it prepared for the D-Day with party taskforces on the carrefours and main thoroughfares late in the evening. The only breaks from the monotony of daily life came from the funerals, the circumcision celebrations, and marriages now more frequent in the rainy season. With their knowledge of politics, college students stood out here and there by their efforts at outreach and explanation. A massive arrival of Guinean nationals from the neighboring countries also sparked excitement and trepidation in anticipation of the "NO" vote and the rupture. The frequency of sermons and prayers in the mosques greeted the arrival of the Great Day, showing beyond the horizon.

Finally, the long-awaited D-Day arrived: Sunday September 28, 1958. In many a locality, Guinea aroused itself from the torpor of the night. As by enchantment, the weather met the occasion, showing its dusky reserves of clouds first early in the morning, and then its finest qualities with an azure blue-sky in mid-day and in the afternoon. The sun shone out radiantly, and the leaves washed by the heavy rains of the season exhibited a verdant luster. Early in the morning, the officials of the administration and the delegates sent by the PDG set up their committees in the polling-places. In villages and in the African sectors of larger towns, a herald reminded the people of the party's directives. Very soon, participation in the election began, massive and orderly. Witnesses were impressed by the organization of the offices, the discipline of the voters, and by the impressive quiet. The skills of the leaders seemed to ease the task of the representatives of the colonial administration. Nowhere were irregularities reported. For instance, in Kankan, Sidikiba Bayo, a leading functionary, supervised the operations across the region from Sanfinah. Everything went smoothly, for voting had become routine for years on end. Still, the absence of music and rejoicing in the courtyards made the day strange and heavy. Worry was etched into people's minds. All they had to do was pass before the polls!

The observation of Guinean witnesses matched those of André

Blanchet, the special correspondent from *Le Monde*. During the day, he visited 40 polling places (!) and noted calm everywhere. He felt that "to know the percentage of the "NO" votes before the polls closed, you needed only to consider the spectacle at the polling places where only African voters were registered."[6] The white ballot-forms for "YES" lay on the ground in the cubicles, scorned by the voters. All those who followed the course of the election in the interior of the country confirmed this testimony. The white ballots for "YES" had no chance; all attention was turned to the mauve "NO" ballot.

In contrast to the votes held before 1956, that were marked by the intervention of the colonial administration, the operations on that day were regular and transparent. No voting fraud was reported. The registered voters took two ballots, mauve and white, into a cubicle, and placed their choice in the ballot-box in the greatest secrecy, behind black curtains. There was no coercion and no vote suppression. That was the watchword from the Political Bureau of the Party. Outside the capital, veterans of the two World Wars and of Indochina could occasionally be recognized, with their uniforms of olive-colored cloth, shiny from age and use, or by their medals fastened to their kaftan. They asked questions about pensions, paid out of Paris, and about fidelity to France and to de Gaulle. Such exchanges brought a note of gaiety to the polling places. And then they could cast their votes.

However, as Blanchet described for certain places in Conakry, and in many villages of the interior, as reported by witnesses, quite often the mauve ballot for the "NO" vote was the only one exhibited, and the vote took place in the presence of a member of the Electoral Committee. These members were indeed zealous! Despite these irregularities, the results matched the expectations, given the deep penetration of the PDG and the presence of the opposition. Just as, a little time later, the old *jeli* Diélikaba Koudounnin Soumano would sing:

> *On September 28, the Elephant wearing mauve seized Kankan hardily,*
>
> *Conquered Beyla, Macenta and Lola,*

---

6. *Ibid*, 181.

Was the victor in Siguiri, Kouroussa, Dabola,

Mastered Dalaba, Mamou and Pita,

Crushed the YES in Boké, Kindia and Conakry

And took the day all across Guinea.

It was a day of Triumph and of Honor

As for the Europeans, there were few of them on the streets, in the café-bars, or even on the beaches where they usually piled up in fine weather. Most of them, no doubt from fear, preferred the safety of their house to the spectacle of the street on that historic day. Their apprehensions stemmed from the fear of becoming objects of irritation to the Africans, and thus, to be tossed in the sea, as was often said in the colonial circles. Those fears were not well-founded, however, for the government of Sékou Touré was opposed to any actions of disorder and violence. That directive, and the presence of soldiers in the towns, may most likely explain why the streets were empty, even in the African quarters. In fact, as soon as people had voted, they hastened back to their compounds. No incidents marked this solemn day of the referendum. Everyone went as planned, in the greatest quiet and dignity, and thus, demonstrating the political maturity of the people and their leaders.

The result of the voting matched expectations. From a total of 1,405,989 registered voters, of whom 1,200,171 voted, the "NO" vote carried the day, tallying more than 94%. Detailed analysis of the vote allowed several pertinent remarks. First, the rate of absenteeism was 15%, a surprising number. Furthermore, the numbers revealed interesting differences, both at the local and regional levels. The results from the cities showed little variation, apart from certain agglomerations at the heart of the Futa-Jallon.

The percentage voting "NO" was uniformly high in the Forest Zone and in Upper Guinea. It varied from 99.99% in Faranah and 95.8% in Kankan. In Maritime Guinea, the percentages counted 99% in Boké, Boffa, and Forécariah, and around 94% in Conakry and 92% in Kindia. The difference was due to the insignificant presence of Europeans and the "assimilated." In the Futa Jallon, the "NO" triumphed, with numbers on the order of 99 % for Dabola, the hometown of the *Député* Diawadou

Barry, for Dinguiraye and Gaoual, and from 92-98% from Pita to Mamou. However, an unexpected variation came with the tallies of Labe (58%), Dalaba (78%), Tougué and Mali (a town in Guinea, not the modern nation): each 80% respectively. These figures stood out as anomalous. The relatively recent movement by the PDG into these areas, the trauma of the suppression of traditional chiefdoms and of the bloody conflicts in Conakry in May, the presence of many veterans, and a certain fidelity to the French ideal—all these factors may help to understand why the results of the vote differed there from the territorial averages. In short, Guinea, under the banner of the PDG and that of the BAG, voted massively against the constitutional project, and issued a categorical "NO" to General de Gaulle.

The Territory now had to face the consequences of its action. On the morning of the Referendum, Jean Risterucci, Governor of Overseas France and Inspector-General of the administrative affairs of the A.O.F., arrived from Dakar on an extraordinary mission. He was a man known for his cleverness and his affability. As soon as the results of the vote were known, on Monday morning, he went to visit Sékou Touré, Chair of the Governing Council, with whom he was well acquainted. The Special Envoy from France needed all his diplomatic talents to communicate the harsh and sharp message he carried. The first diplomatic communication between Paris and Conakry: the note, with no letterhead and without signature, was evidence of a calculated rudeness from the French authorities in direction of the new state of Guinea, as was shown:

The first article of the constitution specifies that the Republic and the peoples of the overseas territories, who, by an exercise of free determination, adopt the present constitution, constitute a Community. By the vote of September 28, the Guinean electorate have refused to adopt the constitution presented for their approval. Through this action, Guinea has separated from the other territories of the A.O.F. that approved the constitution. As a consequence, the constitution will not be applied in Guinea. As a consequence, Guinea no longer enjoys legitimate representation within the Community, whether it be a question of the Metropolitan or the African institutions. Consequently, Guinea can no longer expect the ordinary assistance of the

*Administration of the French state, nor any credit for material
support. Consequently, the responsibilities undertaken by the
French state towards Guinea must be reviewed. So as to avoid
disturbing the administrative and financial operations of the
territory, the public servants under the French state, serving in
Guinea, shall remain for the time being at their posts, but a plan
to transfer these public servants to identical posts in other
territories shall be established and regulated by the High
Commission of the A.O.F., and applied within a period of two
months in progressive and methodical manner. Further, the
suspension of the supply operations will not allow any new
initiatives.[7]*

Guinea had become a pariah, literally punished and banished. France
showed indifference to Guinea's newly acquired independence. The
French authorities were content simply to acknowledge a matter of fact.
In his press conference, following his meeting with Touré, Risterucci
declared that henceforth, "Franco-Guinean relations would be governed
by the principles of international law." Transitional measures would be
jointly taken to avoid, if possible, the sudden interruption of services.

On that subject, Governor Risterucci first gave instructions about the
administrative services. The state services, save for the treasury and agencies for sea and air security, could be transferred to the Guinean government so soon as the latter might make the request, as of October 1.
The French personnel serving in those services would remain available
to Guinea, as technical advisors, for two months or more. As for the
French personnel serving in the Territorial Services, they would also enjoy
a period of two months in which either to sign a contract with Guinea
or to depart. Judicial administration would end, in its current form, on
October 1, and would no longer be carried out in the name of France. The
same applied to all other services. The army would also end its legal existence as of October 1, but it might remain in Guinea for a maximum of
three months. Those Guinean soldiers who so wished might leave it, and
the dates of their availability would be set to avoid disorganizing military
service.

---

7. *Le Monde*, September 30, 1958.

The second category of notifications that Risterucci announced related to economic and financials areas. Henceforth, France would revoke the "most favored nation" status accorded to the importation of Guinean products, as well as the allocation of foreign exchange for new contracts with Guinea financed in foreign currencies. Investments under the FIDES program were suspended, and all activities relating to new projects, such as Konkouré and the rice-growing programs, were also annulled. Active projects would be re-evaluated. The Guinean state would no longer benefit from the assistance of the French budget. Guinea's deficit toward the Treasury of the former Metropolis, totaling some billions of Francs for the fiscal year of 1958, would be negotiated.

The French authorities turned a deaf ear to questions on the independence of Guinea. They refused to make any statement on the formal recognition of the new Guinean state. Under question by the press on the future of the French involved in the private sector of Guinea, following France's withdrawal, the special envoy, Risterucci, in diplomatic tones, offered "There are French in Venezuela, as also in Lebanon, and why not in Guinea?" France's answer, it appeared, had been prepared. This judgment fell like the blade of a guillotine. To the massive "NO" of Sékou Touré's Guinea, de Gaulle's France responded with a categorical "NO" to any notion of normal continuation of Franco-Guinean relations. The vindictiveness involved was thinly veiled. Was such a reaction surprising? Was the reaction from General de Gaulle not evidence, once again, of his sensitivities, if not his attachment to principles, when his government's reaction was devoid of elegance? As Ibrahima Kaké and Saliou Camara point out, emphatically, Guinea was punished, and quite severely.[8] Thus, Guinea became an example for the other colonies!

How did Sékou Touré react to this counterthrust? Witness accounts vary. Some stress his almost febrile state of nerves, others his appearance of determination and calm. On one side, and relying on oral information, Ibrahima Kaké describes Touré as a man bordering on depression, almost an anti-hero. This perspective matches that of H.W. Johnson, a British political analyst, who saw Sékou Touré as a revolutionary against his own will, and a man edging toward psychosis.[9] On the other side, Blanchet,

---

8. Kaké, *op. cit.*, 84-85; Camara, *op. cit.*, 142-160.
9. H. W. Johnson, "Guinea," in John Dunn, ed., *West African States: Failure and Promise* (New York: Cambridge University Press, 1978).

Chaffard, and Lacouture, all journalists, offered more measured opinions. They portrayed the Guinea leader as one who gave "the impression of a somewhat fevered man, tense, perhaps a bit worried, but in no way adopting a position of defiance or the mask of despair."

Their observations come much closer to the opinions of several persons, close to the leader of the PDG, with whom I have had the chance to discuss the matter. The certainty that remains is that General De Gaulle's calculated retort took the Guinean leader by surprise. Yet, Touré was aware of his actions and of their consequences. Serenity was his modus operandi. Therefore, he was deliberate in his steps. The first consequence—a source of pride and of prestige across Africa and internationally—was Guinea's accession to independence, which in Touré's mind represented a major and perfect outcome, a fulfillment of Guinean nationalism. As for the second, involving the possibilities of a break with France: Touré presumed that Guinea's vote would be a blow to de Gaulle. What he played down was that it was also a blow to the great majority of the French who were attached to a specific notion of long-term cooperation between France and Africa.

The "NO" out of Guinea did not touch only one single man, by definition fallible, along with an obviously debatable, and especially perishable, legal text, as Lacouture reported; it also signified the abandonment of a certain conception of inter-racial and supranational cooperation in favor of nationalism.[10] (What did Lacouture make of the many negative votes from the French?) A certain conception of the French *amour-propre* had apparently been wounded. Touré believed that with good will, one might still overcome resentments. Therefore, Chaffard reported:

> *Sékou Touré, for his part, listened to the reading of the note (from the Special Envoy, Risterucci) without reaction.... The announcement of the sanctions made no impression upon him. Did he not plan to quickly negotiate the terms of the association?*

To all appearances, then, Sily remained lucid, and even seemed to exude confidence, for he still believed in a possible plan for association with France. But did those appearances not hide some apprehension? He

---

10. Lacouture, *Cinq hommes et la France*, 358.

found it difficult to believe in a break and in the impossibility of restoring the shattered pots, or to lose faith in the possibilities offered by sovereignty on the international scene.

In a press conference on September 30, the Guinean leader reiterated his intention to associate Guinea with France, in accord with Article 88 of the constitution that stated, "Insofar as it is desired of Guinea." He further affirmed his hope that "France would be the first nation to recognize an independent Guinea, and that she would see to having us recognized by other governments, and to allow us to enter the UN." Those wishes would not come true. Finally, he ended by stating that he was prepared to seek other solutions, should Guinea, despite its good intentions, find itself rejected by the Franco-African group. On October 1, a note from the Ministry for Overseas France gave a foretaste of Paris's answer to the request for association. The message was that there could be no final settlement of the new situation in Guinea until the conclusion of conventions on relations between France and Guinea. Further, certain leaders of Black Africa had already communicated that "in view of the constitution and the reciprocal bonds established among the members of the Community, some decision must be taken on the case of Guinea."

The problem of Guinea was apparently not a priority in Paris. The French authorities consigned it to the realm of Community consultations, to allow Touré's former colleagues to pass judgment on his actions. Speaking about a vote in Guinea in favor of "NO," Houphouët-Boigny stated that "if we are talking about ends in politics, Sékou Touré has abused the commitment of his friends in the RDA, and particularly that of the president of the movement, from whom support and the advice of elders have never been stinted." Most of the African leaders who had voted "YES" made no haste to align themselves with Sékou Touré, nor to smooth his way. In their estimation, "It would be a political error for France to offer any preference to the 'rebels of Conakry'" or to make haste in recognizing the independence of Guinea—the risk was of a trend that might spread. Given the personal animus of General de Gaulle and the resentment of many African leaders, no Franco-Guinean association would soon appear. What to do in the meantime?

History followed its ineluctable course, and events unfolded according to their rules. Sékou Touré, along with his team and the leaders of the opposition, understood that there was no way to move back on their path, and that they must then move forward. A first requirement, answering the aspirations of the people and the new conditions, and fill in the institutional void left by the note from the French government, was to endow the country with a constitution. Thus, the Governing Council summoned the Territorial Assembly to review the situation and take appropriate action. Therefore, on the morning of October 2, 1958, the second day of an independent Guinea, hailed by a large and hopeful crowd, the Assembly met in special session, presided by Saïfoulaye Diallo. The atmosphere was solemn, but also fraught. The audience, assembled in the great hall, under the verandas and out in the street, grasped the importance and the immediacy of the moment.

It was the end of a long and difficult period. No one, even some weeks before, might have foreseen the result of an era marked by violence and unnecessary harm, but also filled with new and enriching ideas, an era in which the peoples, from the Atlantic coast to the mountains in the Forest Zone, realized that they belonged to the same country, and understood, in short, their unity above their diversity. Life had to go on. After September 28, the leaders and the people could discern, in the firmament of history, a new sun, far different from the stars of past days. They greeted the dawn of a new world, a new society, and an imponderable life that might become glorious and magnificent, but that required rapid consecration of its birth. Thus, feelings of a vague nostalgia, of sadness, and of the joy that goes with the rites of passage.

After noting the results of the Referendum, along with the provisions in the French

constitution relating to the vote of territories, the Assembly proclaimed the national independence of Guinea, transformed itself into a Constitutive National Assembly, and accepted the resignation of the administration. Sékou Touré was immediately empowered to create a new government, the first for the Republic; we might note the presence of Diawadou Barry and Ibrahima Barry, called Barry III, appointed respectively to the Ministry of Education and to the Secretariat of State attached to the Presidency, along with that of the Frenchman, Jean-Eugène Mignard in the Ministry of Production. It was a government of national unity, to prevent any attempts at creating disorder based on ethnicity or race. Touré was granted full powers to administer and to pursue the national interests, to engage in and settle all negotiations. Thereafter, the Assembly elected a Commission assigned to draw up a constitution and voted an amnesty for prisoners to mark the fact that the country had achieved independence.

The first messages of diplomatic recognition, sent by Ghana and Liberia, were read aloud to the ovations in the hall, thus creating an atmosphere of pride and festivity. The absence of France from the ceremonies was noted. Nevertheless, Touré and his government paid a courtesy visit to Governor Risterucci, who occupied a palace over which the French tricolor flag still flew. Following this visit, the leader of the government of Guinea sent a telegram to the French President René Coty and to the General de Gaulle to announce that Guinea had declared itself independent and hoping for the establishment of relations.

Paris made no answer. Conakry did not lose hope from that. A second telegram was sent the next week. The answer was a note delivered by an intermediary on a paper with no letterhead or signature. In a dry and condescending tone, mixed with a snide irony, the French authorities asked the new Guinean government to prove its abilities to "effectively ensure the duties and obligations of independence and of sovereignty," and to grant France the time to "consult the agencies of the Community when they have been established." Paris saw no need to rush. Touré now realized that he faced no easy task. He also began to realize his mistake in the matter of the text of the French constitution and the nature of the man, Charles de Gaulle.

Interpretation of the constitution depended not only on the context, but also on the attitude of the person giving the interpretation. Sékou Touré—Sily, and henceforth, the Man of September 28—was dealing with Charles de Gaulle, the Man of June 18, a lawyer taken with himself and with the grandeur of France. De Gaulle responded poorly to a lack of deference. From August 25 on, at the Territorial Assembly of Conakry, the animosity of these two forceful personalities had its effect upon Franco-Guinean relations. This was the start of a flurry of official and officious diplomatic communications between Paris and Conakry. Those problems, and the future of Guinea under Sékou Touré and the PDG, lie outside the focus of our study on the referendum.

On that day, October 2, we must, however, agree that Sékou Touré was resplendent in the glory of heroes called to spectacular actions and to fame. Alas! The irony of fate! The sadness! According to the predictions of the scholar, Karamo Talibi Kaba of Kankan, his aura seemed to be that of a person whose hands were bloodied, his eyes burning with a fire that might consume all before it. In short, the image of a future despot who might sow ruin and desolation or progress and glory in his wake. Guinea would learn it, and history shall judge.

CHAPTER 6
A REFLECTIVE AFTERWORD

FOLLOWING THE MEETING between General de Gaulle and Sékou Touré at the Territorial Assembly of Guinea on August 25, 1958, and the negative vote of the colony in the referendum of September 28, change came gradually to Conakry. De Gaulle's France considered the idea of punishing Sékou Touré, along with his entire country. The way that Guinea achieved sovereignty, under the conditions described in this volume, made their names even more famous. In many countries, in those years, the elites and the youth showed enthusiasm for the new state and raised its leaders to a pinnacle. Their names became famous, illustrious, and memorable—but also, as we must admit, quickly capable lightning strokes of violence and of sinister activities.

In those years, people sang, admired, hailed, and applauded Guinea in a wide range of areas, ranging from political awareness and the popular will to the diversity of its landscape, the promotion of its folklore, and its security. Soon, however, the victims of the affrays of 1955 and 1958 went out into exile. This was the start of a diaspora that soon made Guinean cities out of Dakar, Abidjan, Bamako, Bo, Freetown, Monrovia, and other places. Despite the enchantment of sympathizers from abroad and of Guineans for their independence, Guinea could not manage its situation. The country suffered the painful consequences of independence. The animosity between General de Gaulle and Sékou Touré, evident from the evening of August 25, would continue to define Franco-Guinean relations for many years. Neither diplomacy nor changes of government on either side succeeded in overcoming the feelings of pride, of frustration, and of resentment. In Paris, as in Conakry, both sides were wary, and the diplomats of each country regarded the other with the feelings of the "calico cat and the gingham dog."

Thus, misunderstanding became the norm. France reshaped the institution given the name of Franco-African Community. The organization consisted of the African colonies, without Guinea. On his side, Touré took it ill that his sincere and honest desire for cooperation was ignored. Many complex and lasting difficulties afflicted Guinea. There were frequent blackouts on the urban electric network, shortages of running water for daily use, and deplorable conditions of the roadways, communication systems, hospitals, and schools.

People complained, especially in 2010, some ten years after a government that had the appearance of being democratically elected was established. Citizens complained of their conditions, of the management by former regimes, of the kleptocratic system, of the administrative and financial rigmaroles: in short, of the problems that continue to afflict the country. Difficulties persist. Guineans put their faith in religious belief, while dreaming of better tomorrows and of plans to amend their constitution and to find better ways by which to get along with each other. Therefore, the epilogue to this book on the Referendum of 1958 will highlight the factors that led to bitter fruit. Without demagogy or malice, the analysis will stress the inabilities of the leaders who have governed Guinea, particularly after the changes of regime in 1984 and 2009, but will seek to avoid, as history advises, to open sterile debates.

The history of the first years of Guinea's independence displays pages showing success, failures, and tragedies. Many episodes in this history were violent and painful. Arbitrary imprisonment, the concentration camps of the 1960s, the invasion and hangings of the 1970s, the massacres of the 1980s and of 2009—these are all lugubrious events, hard to ignore. Every regime faced its moments of accomplishment and of atrocity. It seems fair, then, to ask the question: Will Guinea be able to forget? Will she recover from the traumatic experiences of her past? Will she be able to face her future, and, like other countries, develop toward better conditions? Now, sixty-two years old, will Guinea, like any ordinary country, enter a phase of maturity and wisdom?

For a better grasp of the problem, this epilogue looks to aspects of politics, a field that is considered a struggle, sometimes bitter and sometimes moderate, between rivals, such as, in their generations: Sékou Touré, Diawandou Barry and Ibrahima Barry III; Lansana Conté and Diarra Traoré, Alpha Condé, Siradio Diallo, Jean-Marie Doré, Lansana Kouyaté and Cellou Dalein Diallo, and many others, all engaged in the quest for power in the name of an idea of common interest and its associated programs. Thus, the Epilogue leads into a concise review of the past, of the events that unfolded from Independence in 1958, to the era in which democratic change was sparked in 2010.

For practical reasons, and in service to analytic purposes, this review will dwell on the role of the first two regimes; indeed, it is limited to those two regimes, which lasted almost half of a century, and so, offer a historian clear and distinct marker. The presidencies of Sékou Touré and Lansana Conté, while quite different, nevertheless yield landmarks, easy to identify and deserving special attention. These two regimes helped the people of Guinea to grasp the issues of governance or of command, of tolerance, diversity, and unity. The two leaders, despite their differences and individual contradictions, shared the goal of building up the state, and maintaining its unity, along with the jolts, at specific times, required for that plan. They had that feeling for politics. They felt that great national deeds transcended the primacy that some argued should be granted to the simplistic—but soon obsolete—principles of ethnicity or region.

The first president, Sékou Touré, understood himself to be subject to popular choice, despite the rigid, authoritarian, and autocratic image that characterizes the memory of his regime. As for the second, Lansana Conté, his governance was no less rigid, despite the pluralism and liberalism that at the end, he finally tried to adopt. He knew how to turn to, and rely on, military force. He considered it the primordial source of his power. Touré exulted in contacts with the crowd, particularly that of Conakry. Conté took pleasure in military processions, in men with boots and uniforms. He understood their minds and their thought patterns. These two men, Touré and Conté, dominated their periods, each in his own way and with his own modus operandi. One must acknowledge that the system under the PDG and later, under the CMRN (*Comité militaire de redressement national*: Military Comittee for National Revival) put Guinea to the test. For some time, they served as an inspiration and an example. Sékou Touré was the founding father of the nation. He set up its structures and principles, its flaws and its values. He initiated and supported a rigorous control by the state apparatus over people as well as belongings. He marked the mindsets, the habits, the style of dress, and the patterns of thought of the inhabitants. In the eyes of his fellow-citizens, Touré was a symbol of audacity, of the quest for knowledge, and of the severe sanctions against all that might taint the honor of the country. People offered him adulation and preserve the memory of his governance as that of an enlightened but impulsive leader, seething and violent and, therefore, feared because he was expert in the art of proposing ideas that, in appearance, were progressive.

The history of Touré's regime juxtaposes scenes of success, such as the creation of institutions and a political morale, with failures. Touré created schools, medical centers, roads, airports, and factories, but often without much concern for their future maintenance. The president was keen on development and modernization, but also on a respect for authority and obedience. His regime promoted the theater, the arts, and musical performances, and spread their effects through the national culture. This rich development rewarded Guinea with victories in international competitions and festivals. The performers of the ballets and the great bards of Guinea enjoyed renown. Sékou Touré's Guinea also became noted for the strictness of its application of order and honesty in the management of state assets, and of public and individual safety. Along with that repute came horrifying scenes of terror. During the years of independence and decolonization, Sékou Touré and his regime were considered emblematic. In the exercise of his rule, Touré—for reasons that can be linked to the process by which Guinea became independent—displayed the signs of paranoia, fearing plots and invasions, and thus, building prisons and concentration camps. He struck out against anyone suspected of conduct hostile to his regime.

In those years, 1958-1984, the competition between capitalism and communism defined the world. Guinea was rich in natural resources but lacked capital. Therefore, Touré favored the non-capitalist path, seeking monetary independence and, in foreign affairs, non-alignment. With the help of the countries in the Communist bloc, he sought for self-sufficiency in the sectors of agriculture and small businesses. In daily life, Touré practiced simplicity and honesty; however, he remained mute on the weaknesses of his close associates who were entrusted with official responsibilities. He was usually able to defend his actions, vehemently, and to proclaim his opinions, equally vehemently, being so eloquent in the articulation of his thoughts and his form of socialist doctrine. He died on the operating table in Cleveland, OH, in the United States, on March

26, 1984. World leaders acknowledged his position, his grandeur, and his dignity, and many of them also attended his funeral in Conakry to honor him.

Sékou Touré's visit to Washington, D.C., ca. 1982

Lansana Conté was the second president of Guinea. He seized power, and his image is marked by controversy. His regime, at first, inspired fear, but it would later face long processions of the unemployed and protesters in the streets of the capital and the major cities of the interior. These movements served to demystify his authority, for very many of its officials found their prestige erased. The president did indeed offer incendiary statements, such as the famous *Wo nfatara* (Susu: "We were right"), uttered during the crisis of July of 1985, and that led to riots and looting aimed at the property of Mandinka persons. The violence and the pillaging led, in turn, to massacres and to sinister thefts of all sorts. These events accompanied the physical eradication of the trade long associated with the natives of Upper Guinea, and the repression of its cadres in the administration, in horrible scenes. Conté and his lieutenants found it difficult, when traveling on official business outside the capital, to hold their heads high after so many mistakes and examples of incompetence. The regime committed other mistakes, for example in the position it took in February 1996, which led to the firing of Col. Abdourahman Diallo, Minister for Defence. Such blunders weakened its support in Upper Guinea and in the Futa Jallon, the home territories of the two largest ethnic groups in the country. In short, returning to April of 1984, Conté, acting as Deputy Chief of the Army, accepted the idea, along with other officers, of bringing about change, restoring the economy, and managing the country. His team, therefore, seized power on April 4, 1984, some days after the obsequies of Sékou Touré.

Conté proclaimed an admiration for Sékou Touré, saying the latter had treated him well. Nevertheless, he also contradicted himself. It is indeed difficult to explain why he left Touré's widow to molder in prison and had other members of his family sentenced to death. According to rumors that seem relatively plausible, Conté first had to negotiate with the "hawks" of the CMRN. At the start, the committee, chaired by Conté, offered a representative image of the country; the committee seated members from the four regions. However, as is the tradition in praetorian regimes, the members of the junta could not agree among themselves. It was not long before they displayed their frictions and their weaknesses, particularly their regionalism, and their appetite for wealth and luxury. Furthermore, some of them, out of resentment, hoped to destroy the former ruling class.

Conté knew that his education had been rudimentary; he also had a keen sense of the power he had seized. He chose his advisors with circumspection, preferably from close members of his family, or his ethnic group, or from his region, and then from people allied with his cause. It is said that his wives, and particularly Henriette, the first, had much influence over the choice of his cabinet. In such surroundings, he could settle his command. The crisis of July 1985 was an opportunity to arrest and eliminate many officers, native to Upper Guinea, who thus, were potential rivals. Those events led to pillage and political exclusion. The period was an almost unique moment in the modern history of Guinea. Thereafter, Conté launched large-scale programs for agricultural development, which offered another view of his power.

In Maritime Guinea, the palm-groves of Gbantama, of Samaya, of Doty, and the rice plantations of Koba and Bassika and other areas recalled the agricultural past that was a point of pride for Guinea before 1958. The vast rice-growing areas of Norassoba and Mandiana in Upper Guinea also recall the regions that before 1956, the elected officials of the BAG had sought to develop, and that the maestro Fodéba Keita sang in his writings in honor of the Djoliba, the great Niger river. The large and impressive gardening enterprise of Ditinn, near Dalaba in Middle Guinea, offered enormous potential for the development of the production of potatoes, vegetables, and citrus crops for the markets of the Futa, Conakry, and even Senegal. All these points encouraged the rural economy. President Conté invested himself in the land, as they sang. An attachment to the soil, at first particularly in his home coastal region, eventually took over all the parts of Guinea, with farming developments in the Forest Zone.

Conté sought to end the isolation of the countryside and to bring prosperity to those regions. Thus, in part through international assistance, his government became involved in tarring rural roads, along with plans for constructions and for primary schools. The president's plans for development match his image as a "peasant" whose ambition was to make use of the fertile and productive soils of the land. He deserved the title of "customary chief," devoted to his fields.

As such, and as people recall, Conté liked to receive visitors under the *arbre à palabres* (the shade-tree that hosts discussion) in the courtyard of the presidential palace in Conakry. As such, also, he distrusted anything too well-structured, too rational, and too different from the country's culture. Generally, he gave priority to ordinary matters, individual and local, rather than to those of public interest, for he "smelled and loved the earth, the soil, the home," meaning the peasants and ordinary people. This perspective allowed him to understand what "had gone wrong with the system of the PDG," and what had led to a lack of basic staples, the persistence of an illicit market, and the disquiet among the people.

This is no doubt why Conté became a champion of the "market economy," although without joining the monetary zone of the CFA Franc, whose system was based on the French Treasury. However, a market economy generally works properly under transparent political and social rules. Alas, the Guinean system was far from meeting that criterion. The state, whose practices involved rigid structures, was beginning to face serious difficulties. The crisis, ever more immediate, reflected the absence of money in the funds of the Central Bank and the Ministries, in the management of public funds, and in the signing of mining contracts and public markets.

Besides these fiscal symptoms, the country faced an increase in the unemployment rate and the effects of the abolishment of State enterprises, required by the IMF, the World Bank, and other international funding agencies. All these factors made inequality worse and caused great pain—that had not so far been common—across the country. The palpable physiognomy of poverty and want began to appear, slowly, through rural and urban areas. The long-dormant political and social organizations began to engage in protests and demonstrations and to make demands, with ever-increasing frequency. The social harmony disappeared.

Under pressure from social movements and diplomatic missions, bit by bit, the notion of a balanced multi-party system made headway in Guinea, despite the hesitancy of the president, who held a deep dislike for disorder and political agitation. Specifically at the start, the difficulties that faced his regime did not necessarily derive from a lack of funding or foreign assistance, but rather arose from the embezzlement of public money and from fraud in contracts and in the accounting.

Truth be told, the government rarely performed financial audits of its offices. Given such habits, any policy of economic liberalization will find it hard going! This laxity, along with the sinecures, encouraged corruption and spread the extravagant culture of impunity that marked the agents of the various services. Inflation grew, and, in turn, exacerbated the recession. The state suffered a drop in the growth rate. At the beginning of the millennium, the people found themselves impoverished as never before. From this time on, the Conté regime found itself in ever-greater difficulties. Nothing worked properly, except the system of corruption. The economic system became worse because of the demands for structural adjustment that the IMF and the World Bank had begun to include in their agreements with the indebted countries of the Third World. The commercial banks operating around the square in Conakry lacked liquidity. Therefore, the economy of Guinea seized up, while money-laundering and drug-trafficking, winked at by those close to power, increased the costs of living.

In 2004, and specifically in the years 2005-2007, the situation in the interior became bad enough to cause protests in the cities, and agitation in the military barracks, especially in Conakry. At the start of 2007, discontent rose to a crisis. Social distress caused a severe political crisis; under pressure from the unions and organizations of civil society, this led to the nomination of a prime minister with extensive powers, under the watch of the CEDEAO (*Communité des États d'Afrique occidentale*: Community of West African States). This authority, entrusted to the diplomat Lansana Kouyaté, was not provided for in the constitution. It proved difficult to exercise, the more so because Conté had been forced to accept it, and the adulators of the regime took a dim view of the changes. The prime minister quickly lost much of his influence, and the position was abolished. Conté appointed a more docile and complaisant government. However, no progress was made. To the delight of the opposition, in Guinea and abroad, the record of the Conté régime was showing itself clearly, marked by bungling and by corruption. Daily life in Conakry was characterized by the impunity of the major officials and the resurgence of the irrational, accompanied by cohorts of religious sacrifices and with reverence for marabouts and diviners. Thus, it was hardly surprising that regional interest determined the selection of major projects and priorities, such as that of the hydro-electric dam in Garafiri. Nevertheless, and despite all this, some of the fine roads in the country date to the period of Conté's government: particularly the road from Kouroussa to Kankan, crossing the Niger on a bridge, and the road from Kankan to Bamako (in Mali) via Siguiri, both coated with durable asphalt. He was a man of contrasts, and one of his witty critics noted that, "Just as he managed to build with quality, he also managed to destroy and make vanish in quantity."

Therefore—as we must remember, no matter how hard it is to believe—that on the pretext that it showed no profit, he allowed one of his governments to remove and sell the 660 kilometers of rail from the Conakry-Niger Railway, which had been laid down at a cost in sweat and blood during the first decades of colonization. Moreover, the Guinean State received no payment for this monstrous and underhanded transaction: it is another undeniable proof of the corruption of Conté's system. Further, as we should also remember, Conté displayed his skills as a general in 2001, with an outstanding victory in Guéckédougou over the rebels that were vandalizing the peoples in the border regions with Liberia and Sierra Leone, and that sought to destabilize and eventually, overthrow the government of Guinea.

All this means that Conté found it difficult to build up the country and to achieve the great dreams of 1984 and 1986. For a long time, he was president of a state that was adrift and subject to deplorable conditions of governance because his team was so undisciplined. For some years, he was weakened by ailments that ate at him. He turned to specialists, some-times in Guinea, sometimes abroad. The condition brought him down. Conté passed away in December 2008, in Conakry. Immediately follow-ing the announcement of his death, on December 22, a military junta—the CNDD (*Conseil National pour le Développement et la Démocratie*: National Council for Development and Democracy)—took power, sus-pended institutions, and established a new order. Having dissolved the National Assembly, the junta elected Captain Moussa Dadis Camara to the head of government. This new leader was, apparently, popular within one wing of the army. However, he was unknown outside the barracks.

Dadis soon became known through impetuous and incoherent speeches, and through decisions that were equally surprising. People recalled the saying that "a putsch is not aimed at perpetuation the army's control of power, but to cleanse the administration and to organize free, transparent, and democratic elections" in 2010. Dadis added also that "neither he nor any other soldier would seek the presidency." Across the country, people followed the news attentively and regularly on the evening radio broadcasts. They were greatly pleased when the CNDD began its work, which consisted of denouncing malfeasance and remov-ing the perpetrators. In an atmosphere that mixed drama and comedy, Captain Dadis Camara publicly interrogated the former officials sus-pected of theft, embezzlement, and corruption. He had them arrested on the spot. The spontaneity of the language and the unpredictability of the decisions of this tribunal quickly turned the broadcasts into a tragi-comic spectacle. The fate of the accused was only rarely favorable. Furthermore, the Captain's outbursts, his abuse, and his preposterous commentary made his audience—in presence or over the airwaves—laugh. Still, clear-minded citizens quickly recognized something most unusual in the appearances of the Captain and his companions. The traits were worrisome, the more so as he fell under increasing suspicion of tak-ing on the attitude of a tyrant. He proved unable or unwilling to discour-age movements of support (that may have been spontaneous) in some areas. Did Guinea need a future autocrat? Could the CNDD extirpate the roots of Guinea's problems? Could it establish a free and democratic rule of law? With his companions—all of them lieutenants of Conté, rel-atively uneducated and without professional skills—Dadis proved to be terrifying. No doubt, he propounded a form of morality, and it was in appearance honest and almost comparable to that of Captain Jerry Rawlings in Ghana in the 1980s. Still, the actions of the team and their lack of principles created uncertainty.

The Captain's style of public interrogation and forced confessions was known as the "Dadis Show." It increased his popularity, but was it enough to justify a candidacy for the presidency? Such a possibility was a poor match with the expectations of a people thirsting for durable political changes. The situation was grave. The massacre of members of the opposition at the Donka Stadium on September 28, 2009 led to a further tragedy. Following the killings, a member of the Presidential Guard wounded the Captain seriously. Dadis was evacuated abroad for medical treatment. He never returned to Conakry with the title of president. It was an unusual end. Dadis' presidency was proof that good intentions alone are not enough to establish good governance.

His successor, General Sékouba Konaté, another disciple of Lansana Conté, was uninvolved with public business. He left the administration in the hands of high officials and sticky-fingered financial officers. Under his regime, the state treasury was drained at a breath-taking rate. The country experienced many protest movements, some with violence, against the shortages of water and electricity. In general, the protests and the processions in the streets, in urban centers, were turning against the ruling power. Demonstrations quickly took on an ethnic coloring, particularly around Conakry along the northern axis of the Le Prince Road, home to the common people: in Hamdallahi, in Bambeto, from Cosa to Enco 5. Under Konaté, Guinea was, once again, entering the troublesome times of mass marches by the people. The unemployed and the delinquents invaded the major traffic arteries of the towns, acting against whatever sparked their discontent, i.e., the lack of democracy or the opportunity for jobs.

The rule of this atmosphere of instability favored a progressive passage into the civil electoral regime under the pressure of civil society, the unions, and the political parties. Finally, in November 2009, the coalition of the RPG (*Rassemblement du Peuple de Guinée*: Rally of the People of Guinea) with the *Arc-en-Ciel* (Rainbow) led to the election of Alpha Condé to power, a change that launched a new episode in the nation's history. Upon reflection, the problem with Guinea is linked to the idea that the evolution of a society is imponderable, whatever the intentions of, and the precautions taken by, the citizens in their collective action. As is customary, the science of command and nation-building works through unexpected and difficult paths. The individual and social outcome remains deeply unpredictable. The movements of history, then, remain ever surprising to those who would analyze them, for events leading to all sorts of projects may arise and change the plans.

Between 1958 and 2009, Guinea had a good share of surprises. We may note how pluralism affected the social evolution there, in a context marked by the absence of solid traditions of governance and by the lack of financial resources. Therefore, people applauded the startling and unexpected national response of the peoples carried by enthusiasm over the Referendum of 1958. Their response in unison to the challenge laid down by General de Gaulle was the seed of a great dream that remains unfulfilled. The upheavals that occurred under the regimes of Touré, of Conté, and their successors are evidence of the persistence of difficulties, and that confirm the thought that "a state is almost as fragile as a human life," with its almost surprising, unavoidable, and unforeseen eventualities. Indeed, Guineans are now wondering about their state, their ruler, and his team, and their scheme to perpetuate their regime. Who could they believe? President Alpha Condé, who strongly fought for fairness, democracy, and justice, under the former regimes, has now established his own autocratic system under his RPG party that is, too, riddled with incompetence, bad governance and embezzlement of public funds in the midst of unprecedented pauperization! The country is experiencing a horrible and astounding crisis. In conclusion, in Guinea, one never knows. The country, awash with potentialities, needs to draw, along its fervent prayers, upon its most vital energies to escape the despotism and stagnation from which it has suffered for decades.

BIBLIOGRAPHY

Jean-Paul Alata, *Prison d'Afrique* (Paris: Seuil, 1976)

B. Ameillon, *La Guinée, bilan d'une indépendance* (Paris: Maspéro, 1964)

Yves Bénot, *Idéologies des indépendances africaines* (Paris: Maspéro, 1969)

André Blanchet, *Uitinéraire des partis africains depuis Bamako* (Paris: Plon, 1958)

Laye Camara, *Dramous* (Paris: Plon, 1966)

Robert Bourgi, *Le général de Gaulle et l'Al'rique noire* (Dakar: NEA, 1980)

Sylvain Soriba Camara, *La Guinée sans la France, Presses de la Fondation nationale des sciences politiques* (Paris: Presses de la Fondation nationale des Sciences politiques, 1976)

Georges Chaffard, *Les carnets secrets de la décolonisation, tome 2* (Paris: Calmann-Lévy, 1967)

Alpha Condé, *Guinée, Albanie d'Afrique ou néo-colonie américaine* (Paris: Editions Git-le-cœur., 1972)

Charles de Gaulle, *Fil d'épée... Mémoires d'espoir, tome 1* (Paris: Plon, 1970)

Alpha Abdoulaye Diallo, *La vérité du minister* (Paris: Calmann-Lévy, 1985)

Alpha Diawara, *Guinée* (Dakar: Cerda, 1967)

Ansoumane Doré, *Économie et société en République de Guinée (1958-1984) et perspectives* (Paris: Editions Bayardère, 1986)

Victor DuBois, *The Guinean Vote for Independence: The Maneuvering Before the Referendum of September 28, 1958* (New York: AUFS, 1962)

Lansiné Kaba, *La Guinée dit "NON" a de Gaulle* (Paris: , 1989)

Lansiné Kaba, "The Guinean Politics: A Critical Historical Overview," *Journal of Modern African Studies* 15 no. 1 (1977): 25-45.

Ibrahima Baba Kaké , *Sékou Touré, le héros et le tyran* (Paris: J. A. Livres, 1987)

Sidiki Kobélé Keita, *Le PDG, artisan de l'indépendance nationale en Guinée, 1947-1958* (Conakry: INRDG, Bibliothèque nationale, 1978)

Sidiki Kobélé Keita, *Ahmed Sékou Touré, homme du 28 septembre 1958, 2ND edition* (Conakry: INRDG, Bibliothèque nationale, 1977)

Sako Kondé, *Guinée : le temps des fripouilles* (Paris: La Pensée universelle, 1974)

Jean Lacouture, *De Gaulle, vol. 2* (Paris: Seuil, 1985)

Jean Lacouture, *Cinq hommes et la France* (Paris: Seuil, 1961)

Jacob Moneta, *Le PCF et la question coloniale, 1920-1965* (Paris: Maspéro, 1971)

Ruth Sach Morgenthau, *Political Parties in French Speaking West Africa* (New York: Oxford University Press, 1964)

Yves Person, *Samori, une révolution dyula* (Dakar: IFAN, 1968)

Roland Pré, *L'avenir de la Guinée française* (Conakry: Editions guinéennes, 1951)

Claude Rivière, *Mutations sociales en Guinée* (Paris: Marcel Rivière et Cie, 1971)

Paul-Henri Siriex, *Houphouët-Boigny* (Dakar: Nathan/NEA, 1986)

Jean Suret-Canale, *La République de Guinée* (Paris: Editions sociales, 1970)

Ahmed Sékou Touré, *L'action politique du PDG* (Paris: Présence africaine, 1959).

Ahmed Sékou Touré, *Expérience guinéenne et Unité africaine* (Paris: Présence Africaine, 1959)

INDEX